OF UNA JEFFERS

# OF UNA JEFFERS

BY

Edith Greenan

*Edited and Introduced by*
*James Karman*

Story Line Press
*1998*

Published by Story Line Press
Three Oaks Farm
P.O. Box 1108
Ashland, OR 97520-0052


This publication was made possible thanks in part to the generous
support of the Andrew W. Mellon Foundation, the Charles Schwab
Corporation Foundation and our individual contributors.

*Book design by Chiquita Babb*


Library of Congress Cataloging-in-Publication Data

Greenan, Edith, 1896–1980.
    Of Una Jeffers / by Edith Greenan; edited and introduced by
James Karman.
        p.   cm.
    Includes index.
    ISBN 1-885266-64-2
    1. Jeffers, Una, 1884 or 5–1950. 2. Jeffers, Robinson, 1887–1962
—Marriage. 3. Poets, American—20th century—Biography.
4. Authors' spouses—United States—Biography. I. Karman, James.
II. Title.
PS3519.E27Z63   1998
811'.52—dc21                                               98-36930
    [b]                                                      CIP

# Contents

*La Dame à la Licorne:* "A mon seul désir"
Paris, musée du Moyen-Age—Cluny
© Photo RMN

# Introduction

## *Mon Seul Désir*

At the Cluny Museum in Paris, there is a suite of six *mille-fleurs* tapestries known collectively as *La Dame à la Licorne*—"Lady with the Unicorn." Though no one knows for sure what they represent, they seem to offer an allegory of the five senses. In the first tapestry, a regal woman holds a mirror before a unicorn, a gesture which probably denotes Sight. In the second, she plays an organ, which seems to depict Hearing. Three more tapestries have scenes which apparently represent Touch, Smell, and Taste—but all of this is conjecture. Clearly, though, with the flowers and trees and animals that fill the weavings, they are meant to celebrate the beauty of this world and the sumptuous pleasure that comes with living in a garden of delight. The sixth tapestry presents a problem, however. If the scheme so far is correct, what could the "sixth sense" be? The scene itself is enigmatic: a courtly lady comes forth from a blue pavilion, the flaps of which are held open by a lion on her right and a unicorn on her left. A lady-in-waiting stands beside her holding a chest into which the lady seems to be placing a necklace. Above her, emblazoned on the tent, are the words *"mon seul désir"*—"my only desire" or "my sole desire." Before these words, there seems to be a letter "*a*" and after them another letter, possibly "*p*." Some art historians add the "*a*" to the motto, which turns it into a salutation—"to my sole desire"—but no one knows for sure if this is right or even what the motto means.

A photograph of this very tapestry hangs in a special place in Una Jeffers' room on the second floor of Hawk Tower—right where she left it more than half a century ago. Photographs of the other five tapestries hang nearby, taking their places among other *objets de vertu* in a room that reverberates with romance. Paneled in a warm red Japanese oak, the room contains a melodian, a Spanish day bed, and numerous family heirlooms and artifacts: a copy of the Wedgewood Portland vase that belonged to Jeffers' father, an autographed portrait of Yeats, dried leaves from the trees near Shelley's grave in Rome, a wax figurine regarded by Una as a madonna, a Babylonian tile inscribed with a prayer to Ishtar, a small stone head of a sacred dancer from the Angkor temples in Cambodia, and so on. The room has oriel windows that look out upon the sea; it can be reached from the inside through a secret passage that twists up from the room below and from the outside from steps that continue upwards to two open platforms above. Over the fireplace in Una's room is a Latin motto, "Ipsi sibi somnia fingunt"—"They make for themselves their own dreams"—and over the doorway, on the outside, is a sandstone carving of a unicorn.

Desire, dreams, unicorns—all three were woven into Hawk Tower and Tor House, the extraordinary estate that Robinson and Una built for themselves on the seacoast of Carmel. Una, as lady of the demesne, helped her husband create a defiantly pre-modern sanctuary where fireplaces created the only warmth and oil lamps the only light, and life could be lived as it had been for centuries. Her sensibilities in this regard were similar to those of the Pre-Raphaelites and the devotees of the Arts and Crafts movement in England and America. She sought a natural, purposeful, aesthetically beautiful life that was guided from within, rooted in tradition yet free of its constraints, civilized but ever open to renewal from the ancient wellsprings of myth, magic, and mystery.

Among the many animal guides that helped her on her own life's journey, the dog was especially important. Una had a special affinity for English bulldogs, and Tor House was never for long without one. Insofar as the world of the imagination was concerned, the unicorn was preeminent. In pictures, figurines, and other artifacts—most of which were given to Una by friends—unicorns enlivened Una's home.

Edith Greenan mentions this in *Of Una Jeffers*, the loving memoir reprinted here. And the original book itself, handsomely crafted by Ward Ritchie in 1939, uses a unicorn as an emblematic motif. A drawing of a rearing unicorn appears on the jacket, the cover, and the title page.

What is the story behind *Of Una Jeffers?* What sixth sense or "sole desire" in Edith's heart prompted her to write it? And how does this new edition compare to the first one?

The story, of course, begins with Edith herself. In 1936, in her early forties, she entered a period of self-scrutiny. She was the wife of James Greenan, a successful mining engineer, and the mother of three children—Maeve, James, and Owen. She was living well in the Philippines and, though healthy and happy, was troubled by a feeling that she had lost her way. Something was missing in her life—what, she did not know. To find out, she left her husband, only temporarily she thought at first, and returned to the United States. She took her children to Carmel and reentered the life of her admired friend, Una.

Edith and Una were more than friends. They not only shared a special affection for each other but they also shared an experience —a crucial, central experience for both of them. Both had once been known as "Mrs. Edward G. Kuster."

The basic facts of the story are probably well known to many who read this book. When Una met Robinson she was already married to "Teddie" Kuster, an attorney in Los Angeles. In order to salvage the marriage, after her affair with and love for Robinson was exposed, Una agreed to travel by herself in Europe for a few months. She and Teddie hoped that time apart from each other would give them both a chance to sort through their problems. They also hoped that Una's separation from Robinson would allow their relationship to cool and, like an untended fire, die out. The plan did not work, however. Letters exchanged between Teddie and Una—earnest, hopeful, recriminatory, resigned—gave them a chance to slowly, at a distance, talk themselves out of their marriage without the pain and bitter anger that daily contact might have brought. Besides, though separated from Robinson, embers still burned in Una's heart; when she returned and found her way to him once again, the fire flared up all the higher.

It was during this time—1912, while Una was in Europe—that Teddie met Edith. She was sixteen, a schoolgirl in Bakersfield, helping her father in his law office. And therein lies another story.

To start from the beginning—or rather *a* beginning—Edith was born October 8, 1896, in Sisson, California, later known as Mount Shasta. Her mother, Margaret Jane Wooden, lived with her family there on a ranch. Her father, Elias James Emmons, met Margaret during a visit to Sisson; according to family legend, he fell in love with her the first time he saw her singing in a church choir. He was living down the valley in Chico, where he served as assistant district attorney. The couple soon married and eventually settled in Bakersfield. They had two children, Elias Carroll and Edith June.

Emmons remained in politics and quickly rose through the ranks. He served as district attorney in Bakersfield, then entered the state legislature, first as a representative and then as a senator. He was popular, prosperous, and powerful—the very epitome of a California self-made man.

His life took a turn, however, in 1905. As Chairman of the Committee on Commissions and Retrenchments, a special committee established to investigate improprieties in the real estate mortgage business, he had subpoenaed the books of the Continental Building and Loan Association. William Corbin, the secretary of Continental, refused to provide them; accordingly, he was called before the full body of the senate to answer charges of contempt. On the day of the hearing, Corbin's attorney surprised everyone by saying that his client ignored the committee because the committee itself was corrupt. Emmons and three other senators, the attorney charged, were guilty of accepting bribes. Pandemonium was unleashed. "Here was a bomb loaded with scandal," said the newspapers, "and when it burst the Senate seemed to reel with the shock." The accused senators looked at each other in amazement. Emmons, his "face white as marble," rose to deny the charges. He no doubt knew at that very moment, however, with crushing certainty, that his fate was sealed. Forces were aligned against him that would be very difficult to combat, powerful forces that, like the strands of a web, came at him from every direction and tied him tighter and tighter in a knot.

The *San Francisco Call*, reporting the story on January 31, 1905 (though the events happened the day before), attests to some of its scope:

> The breaking of to-day's scandal marks the beginning, politicians say, of the greatest war that has ever been waged between public officials and private enterprises, and will mark decisive defeat of one or the other of the factions that have kept the Democracy of California a divided force since the first days of Phelan's ascendency. On one side are arrayed Gavin McNab, Washington Dodge, Franklin K. Lane and all the Bourbons that so battered William R. Hearst for unanimous endorsement by the Santa Cruz convention for President of the United States. Against them are William R. Hearst and the fragment of the Democratic machine he controls.

This was a political, cultural, and media battle of the first magnitude—not just between public officials and private enterprise, but between sub-factions and personalities of every sort. And Emmons was caught in the middle of it all.

His worst fears were soon realized. With the newspapers sensationalizing the story virtually every day, he lost his seat in the senate. A few months later, he was convicted and sent to prison. As time passed, though, and new questions were raised, it became clear to more and more people that Emmons had been treated unfairly. In 1910, at the urging of Republicans, Democrats, a superior court judge, and others involved, he was given a full pardon. He returned to Bakersfield and resumed a law practice which grew steadily over the years and became ever more distinguished. When he died in 1927, his obituary in Sacramento described him simply as "a widely known attorney and former state senator from Kern county who won fame in both civil and criminal court practice." His death was still front page news in the *San Francisco Chronicle,* but there, too, he was described simply as a "noted lawyer," a "famous criminal attorney" who had once served in state government. No mention was ever made of his earlier misfortunes. For whatever reason—respect for Emmons, regret for what happened to him, amnesia—the matter was dropped.

Edith never forgot. The event that disrupted her childhood pressed upon her from within and forever shaped her life. She loved her father, idolized him, and wanted to do everything she could to help him. That is why, in 1912, she occasionally worked in his office—filing, typing, and greeting clients.

One day, during this time, an affluent, socially prominent attorney from Los Angeles stopped by. He was Teddie Kuster, in Bakersfield on business. After chatting with Edith for awhile, he asked if she would help him type a letter. The friendship that ensued from this brief meeting soon turned into courtship. Before long, Edith moved to Los Angeles to be near Teddie and immersed herself in the lively culture there. She enrolled in the Girl's Collegiate School where she studied music.

It is impossible to say exactly what forces drew the two together. For Edith, the urgency of love and the chance to leave home and start out on her own were positive inducements. For Teddie, love was a factor, too. But he was over twice Edith's age and he was still married to Una, who was in Europe at this time sorting out her own conflicted feelings.

When Una returned and the inevitable divorce was announced, it was something of a scandal. Because of Kuster's social standing, the *Los Angeles Times* gave generous coverage to the story, complete with photographs of everyone concerned. Kuster expressed his bitterness over the breakdown of his marriage—blaming it mostly on Una's acceptance of new ideas, especially those concerning the autonomy of women. Tolstoy and Ibsen were mentioned, and comments were made about Una's willful role in making theirs a childless home. But he wished Una well and expressed an earnest desire for everyone's happiness. The headline for the story which appeared February 28, 1913, was also hopeful: "Love's Gentle Alchemy to Weld Broken Lives." The kicker provides more detail: "Amazing Story of Kuster Separation Comes to Light With Attorney's Admission that He Will Wed Another as Soon as Decree Is Final." That, in fact, is what happened. The legal dissolution of the marriage occurred August 1, 1913. Robinson and Una, anxious to begin their life together, were married the very next day. Rather too emphatically, so were Edward and Edith.

Though Robinson and Una immediately embarked upon a life of creativity and accomplishment, Edward and Edith foundered. They tried hard to make a life together, but within a few years their marriage failed. Even so, this was a golden time for Edith. With Edward's help and encouragement, with the circle of friends and relationships he drew her into, she escaped the sorrows of her childhood and began to blossom as a woman.

Had Edith not married Kuster, she never would have met Una —and Una proved to be, as Jeffers himself says in his prefatory note to *Of Una Jeffers*, the pole-star by which Edith navigated life's trackless sea.

*Of Una Jeffers* begins in 1912 with Edith, acutely nervous, on her way with Edward to meet Una for the very first time. From there it jumps around, guided only by the internal logic of association and memory, to the years after her divorce from Edward when they could talk as friends, to her childhood in Bakersfield (with no mention of her father), to the early years of her marriage to James Greenan and the birth of their three children, to her intimate friendship with Una and Robinson and the experiences they shared from 1912 to about 1922. The book draws to a conclusion with Edith's return to Carmel in 1936 after a long absence and ends with her thoughts at the moment she was writing—in the fall and winter of 1938 and the spring of 1939. As Edith worked on the book, she was just coming to the realization that her sixteen-year marriage to Greenan was finished; indeed, they were divorced the next year. So her heart's moon was waning, a dark time was slowly setting in, she was thinking about love—how precious it is, how easily lost—and she was hoping, by returning to a moment when her heart waxed full, to find her way to some renewal.

Una was the key to this. Edith looked up to her—like a daughter to a glamorous mother, or a younger sister to an older. Una, twelve years older, was a guardian figure in Edith's psyche, a guide who represented all she hoped to be. And Una's marriage to Robinson, which Edith witnessed in "the first ecstasy of love fulfilled," was for her the very model of romantic bliss. From the beginning of her memoir, therefore, where Edith describes Una as a Botticelli madonna with skin like jasmine petals, to the end, where Una wears a madonna-blue dressing-gown and sits combing her hair by the fire, Una's portrait is idealized.

But the portrait is no less real for that. Much of the charm of Edith's book, in fact, lies in its unabashed warmth and admiration; much of its value, furthermore, lies in its simple, unstudied description of events. Edith was close to Una when Una gave birth to her first child, a daughter named Maeve who only lived for a day; she visited Una regularly for extended periods of time when she moved to Carmel; she watched how she created a life for herself and Robinson there, first in a little cabin in the woods, then in a brown-shingled bungalow, and finally in Tor House; she observed the glow of motherhood in Una when the twins were born; and she saw how Una nurtured, indeed inspired, Robinson's creative genius. Her recollections and impressions, therefore, provide essential information about Una's and Robinson's crucial early years.

Her recollections also provide information about herself—and this helps us better understand the significant but mostly hidden role she played in the Jeffers home. A beautiful little story that Edith tells about Una's parents is helpful here. When they were courting, Una's father took her mother for a sleigh ride in the Michigan snow. Una's mother was wearing a blue chiffon veil which the wind suddenly blew off and carried away. A long time later, after they were married, they found wisps of the veil woven into a bird's nest in their garden. In the same way, wisps of Edith's personality and influence show up in the record of Una's and Robinson's life and in some of Jeffers' poems.

"Fauna," for instance, is a poem which includes an image inspired by Edith. The poem was written very early in Jeffers' career, sometime between 1915 and 1918. Set on the seacoast of Carmel, it tells the story of a young man who is on fire with love for a dark-skinned (sun-tanned) woman from southern California. A code of honor forbids him to pursue her for she is already married—she is described as "a gold-ringed wife and childless." Thinking he is alone on the shore, he bemoans his passion. He is overheard, however, by a fair-skinned woman named Nais who scoffs at his scruples. Since, for her, Eros should never be constrained, she even offers herself as a lover. Though the young man at first declines the invitation, he soon submits. At dawn, still lying in Nais' arms, he is visited by the very Goddess of Love herself, who blesses the lawless union. Emboldened and unbridled, he then pursues Fauna, the true object of his ardor. When she submits, after coyly prolonging the moment of seduction, flower petals from all over the world rain down upon the couple as they lie happily entwined in their tree-embowered bed.

Though much has been made of this poem, especially concerning its possible autobiographical significance, it seems best to read it as Jeffers intended—as a romantic narrative written in conscious imitation of an idyll penned by Theocritus, the Hellenistic master. As such, it is a poem about "innocent" love fulfilled. Fauna, the title character, is a dancer whose ankles are bitten by the soft white waves of the sea when she dances on the shore in the moonlight—and this is where Edith comes in. As she says in her memoir, she often took walks with Robinson and Una on the beach and, as they watched, she would sometimes leap and play in the surf. Robin once told her that she skimmed "the water like some beautiful sea bird" and that he would "never go to the shore again without seeing a bacchante along the edge of the foam." Una said specifically that Edith "had helped Robin to the vision of Fauna, dancing ankle-deep, in the lapping waves."

It is important to add here that Edith's movements, however playful and spontaneous, were highly disciplined and no doubt beautiful to watch. She was, after all, a serious student (and later a teacher) of dance. Indeed, she was a pupil at Denishawn School—the legendary institution established in 1914 by Ruth St. Denis and Ted Shawn, perhaps the two most influential figures in the early history of modern dance. Martha Graham and Doris Humphries were Edith's classmates at Denishawn at the very moment when the school was reaching its peak of creative power; with them she learned the revolutionary steps and gestures, the ways of moving musically about in space, that produced a whole new form of bodily expression.

In this regard, it seems likely that Edith helped Jeffers visualize the powerful dance scene in *Tamar*—where, on the seashore in the moonlight, Tamar at first dances "with slow steps and streaming hair" and then, as a preternatural chant becomes more primal, gives in to wantonness and wild gestures. Tamar thrashes and twists until her feet are dashed with blood and she falls down gasping on the tide-line. Native dances with pounding rhythms, sometimes building to orgiastic frenzy, were a part of the Denishawn repertoire. St. Denis herself had created her reputation with exotic interpretations of ethnic dances and performed such pieces as "Chitra Hunting" and "The Garden of Kama." Shawn at this time—in step with the trend that made primitivism a key feature of modern art—choreographed such works as "Earth Cycle," "Nature Rhythms," "Savage Dance," and "Les Mystères Dionysiaques." Edith would have learned these dances—if not the actual pieces, then the spirit that informed them and the movements that comprised them—and she probably shared them with her friends. For certain, after a trip to Hawaii in 1918, where she studied native dances, Edith and two companions performed for Robinson and Una in Tor House. On a moonlit night, in costume, they danced Tamar-like for hours, growing "more excited as the night wore on" and quitting only after the sleeping twins, early in the morning, began to cry. At one point, as Una clapped her hands to the beat of the drums and Robinson watched, one of Edith's supple friends "bent backward to pick a scarf from the ground with her teeth."

Other evidence of Edith in Jeffers' poems is more fleeting. In *Cawdor* he uses her name, but whether he has Edith herself in mind is impossible to say. Early in the poem, when Fera is striking a marriage bargain with Cawdor, she says to her father "you remember Edith" and describes her as a friend who "had fine dreams" but lacked her own energy and passion. In a similar instance, according to a story Edith told her daughter, Jeffers once asked her for a name, different from her real one, which he could use in a poem. Edith said "Alma" and soon thereafter Jeffers began work on "Point Alma Venus"—a poem which he never finished but which he used as the basis for *The Women at Point Sur*.

Traces of Edith in Una's life are more difficult to discern—not because they are less significant but because the most important ones are hidden more deeply in the heart. Like all close friends, Edith and Una were affected, in ways even they could not fully understand, by those spontaneous expressions of sympathy and affection, "those little, nameless, unremembered acts/Of kindness and of love," as Wordsworth calls them, that shape lives beneath the surface and bind souls together in intimate communion.

One such act of kindness and of love was Edith's naming of her first child, a daughter born October 25, 1924. She named her Maeve, in memory of the daughter Una and Robinson lost. Who can say how much this quiet gesture helped heal a wound that still caused pain? For her part, Una treated Maeve like a godchild. Once, when Maeve was about sixteen, Una gave her a prized moonstone, the first one she and Robinson found on a beach near Carmel. Una had a jeweler attach a small gold loop to it so it could be worn as a necklace. Another time, she gave Maeve two heirloom Staffordshire figurines—a lady with a dove perched upon her wrist and a gentleman holding a lute.

Another act of kindness and of love, generous and lasting, was Edith's decision to write *Of Una Jeffers*. When she first conceived the project, her "sole desire" was simply to tell the story of her famous friend. But desire is a cord plaited with many threads, some of which are hidden. As mentioned previously, Edith was unsettled at the time she worked on the manuscript. Her marriage was disintegrating and, feeling she had lost her way, she was searching for a path to inner peace and happiness. Writing about the past— her own and Una's blossoming—brightened the present and gave hope to the future. This was something Una needed, too. Indeed, if the fall and winter of 1938 and the spring of 1939 were dark for Edith, they were nearly pitch-black for Una. Still recovering from an attempted suicide, she was struggling through what was doubtlessly the very worst moment of her life.

In the summer of 1938, the Jeffers family—Robinson, Una, Garth, and Donnan—vacationed as usual at Mabel Dodge Luhan's house in Taos, New Mexico. Jeffers was in extremely low spirits at the time. He had just turned fifty, writing had become difficult for him and, though he tried not to pay attention to critics, he knew more and more of them were denouncing, even ridiculing, his work. Even Carmel was bothering him. The streets and beaches were filled with tourists, and social engagements interfered with his need for solitude. Mabel, ever the meddler, thought Robinson might benefit from the attention of a younger woman and arranged it so that he and an attractive musician could have time together. For Una, whether anything physical occurred hardly mattered. She was devastated by the simple fact of Robinson's emotional betrayal. He had succumbed to the woman's blandishments and listened when she said that Una herself might be the cause of his declining creativity and general distress. Dreamwalking in despair, Una got into a bathtub to keep her blood from splattering, put a pistol to her heart, and pulled the trigger. The bullet glanced off a bone, traveled around her ribcage, and exited from her back. After a week or so in the hospital, she and Robinson and their two sons left Taos and returned home to Carmel. Una's body healed quickly but her spirit was broken.

At just this moment, Edith began work on her memoir. Seen within this context, her desire to write about Una's and Robinson's early days together seems to have come as much from her concern for Una, perhaps more so, as from concern for herself—which makes the manuscript itself all the more poignant.

Edith told Una that the idea for the book came to her early in the summer, just as the trip to Taos was getting underway. Perhaps, like some of Una's other friends, she knew by her sixth sense that trouble was in the air. Work began in earnest late in the summer, after Una's return, and continued through the fall. Edith, in no way a professional writer, hired a man named Harvey Taylor to help her; he told her he had worked on a similar project concerning Elinor Wylie. His expertise proved negligible, however, and Edith continued for the most part on her own through the fall of 1938. In January, Marcella Burke, a close friend of both Edith and Una, came to Carmel. She stayed with Edith for over a month and helped bring the book to final shape.

Throughout this time, while her own house was being built, Edith lived in a rented home just up the street from Una, only a hundred yards or so away. This meant that she saw Una virtually every day and, as she recorded her memories, apprised her of progress and solicited help. Herein might be found the true purpose and value of the book for, however much publication might have pleased Edith and Una, the time they shared recalling happy days most certainly helped Una heal. Indeed, all the while Una thought she was helping Edith, Edith, ever so softly—talking, listening, writing things down—was soothing Una's wounded heart.

She also tempered Robinson. By involving him in the project, even if only a little, Edith gently led him back to where he started —to the early years of his marriage. This enabled him to see again, with renewed appreciation, the beauty and strength of the woman he loved. At some point, Edith must have asked him to write answers to several questions or to record a series of thoughts. Among her papers there is a note in his hand which reaffirms his own recently published description of Una. The paragraph is written in the third person, as if Edith had written it herself.

> You remember what he wrote about her last year, in the preface to his Selected Poems—'She excited and focused my nature, gave it eyes and nerves and sympathies. She is more like a woman in a Scotch ballad, passionate, untamed and rather heroic—or like a falcon—than like any ordinary person.' That is quite a thing for a man to say about his wife, after 25 years of marriage.

This paragraph must have been passed to Una, perhaps by Robinson himself, for one in her hand makes use of it. Una's version, also written in the third person, is more expansive.

> There can be no shadow of a doubt as to Una's influence upon Robin's work. You remember years ago he said that the lines

Wordsworth wrote about his sister Dorothy would describe himself & Una. These lines: 'she gave me eyes, she gave me ears,' &, Robin added, 'arranged my life.' And last year he wrote of her in the Preface to his 'Selected Poetry'—'She excited & focused my nature, gave it eyes & nerves & sympathies. She is more like a woman in a Scotch ballad, passionate, untamed & rather heroic—or like a falcon—than an ordinary person.' That is quite a thing for a man to say about his wife after 25 years of marriage.

Neither paragraph was used by Edith. Surely, though, the act of writing them was therapeutic. Una certainly needed to hear these words from Robinson, she needed to see them and say them out loud—for they were the ones which established her identity and, to a large extent, defined her place in the world.

Robinson needed to say and see them, too. At the very least, they—and others like them—reminded him of all that was most precious in his life, all that was in danger of being lost. Though it is impossible to gauge the full impact of Edith's project on his understanding of himself and his marriage, the effect was clearly substantial. In his prefatory note, written after he read the finished manuscript, he admits to being deeply moved by the recaptured beauty of earlier years. He also refers to "the undeserved good fortune" that followed him after he met Una. An unpublished draft for this note is housed in the Humanities Research Center at the University of Texas, Austin. Therein, he affirms the past and present: "We lived a golden time in those days. Our time is still golden." He also reveals more feeling: "after I had read the book I sat thinking, joyfully and painfully, thinking that I have never deserved the good fortune I have had in life and in love." He places Edith's memories in the larger scheme of things where, though ultimately unimportant, they become a part of the universal order, a "part of the truth." Finally, he describes a late night walk outdoors where, with Edith's recollections in mind, he "watched Orion and Sirius go down, and the Dipper over the house." Humbled before the cosmos, pensive and alone, he returns home.

Una had already gone to bed, he says, "and after the eighth tumblerful of California Burgundy I wrote some verses. Verses that are too narrowly personal, and of the mood of the moment, to be reprinted in any book of mine."

Whatever he said to himself in the mood of that moment—after reading Edith's book, after walking beneath the stars, after drinking eight full glasses of truth-telling wine—is lost to us. But he said something, and the scars from Taos eventually faded away.

Jeffers' midnight walk along the shore occurred in late February or early March. The final draft of Edith's manuscript, which includes his prefatory note, is dated March 5, 1939. This version was sent to Ward Ritchie in Los Angeles and published by him in June, 1939.

Ritchie's design for the book featured heavy rag paper with torn edges, drawings by Fletcher Martin, five photographs, blue cloth binding imprinted with silver, and a light brown jacket with title and decorations in blue. Though the edition was small—only two hundred fifty copies were printed—it attracted nationwide attention. The American Institute of Graphic Arts, located in New York, named *Of Una Jeffers* one of the best "Fifty Books of the Year" based on presentation and subject matter.

Edith's memoir sold out immediately and was never reprinted—until now. The published text is offered here virtually verbatim. It includes, along with the memoir itself, a dedication and a prefatory note by Edith, Jeffers' comment, three poems that were unpublished at the time of printing, and a letter from Una written in response to the memoir after it was completed.

This edition differs from the original, however, in three important ways. First, the number of illustrations has increased from five to twenty-three. Three of the original photographs have been retained—"Una Jeffers" by Johan Hagemeyer, "Una at the Villa d'Este," and "Edith and Una and Billy." "Haig of Bemersyde" has been dropped and a different portrait of Una by Arnold Genthe has been substituted. Second, this edition includes an index. And third, selections from an early draft of the manuscript are provided.

Of the three changes, the latter is the most significant. Edith's early draft, typed and corrected in pencil, is kept in the Greenan family archives. Though less polished, it contains substantially the same material. Countless details are different, however, and, by comparing one version of an anecdote to another, it is possible to see how Edith's memory and insight evolved—as it was sharpened and corrected by Una, Robinson, Marcella, and other friends. The notes which appear in the text refer to corresponding or related passages in the earlier draft. The passages themselves follow the main text in a separate section titled "Selections from an Early Draft" which begins on page 72.

Edith lived near Una through the turbulent war years of the 1940s; she left Carmel just before Una died in 1950. With two brief marriages before James Greenan (with whom she had her only children) and two after, she was married five times. Ever willing to take risks, impulsive at times, she was loved by those who knew her as a vital, affectionate woman, ready with laughter, ready with tears. In 1956 she returned alone to Sacramento—her father's Calvary, and in some deep ways her own—where she lived with her daughter Maeve until she died in 1980.

Though Edith outlived Una by thirty years, she never outgrew her feeling of devotion. Perhaps because she was so young when she met her, so achingly self-conscious, she remained forever a lady-in-waiting, gratefully and happily so—like the maiden in the sixth tapestry of the "Lady with the Unicorn" series who serves the central figure.

To return to that mysterious tableau: no sky, no horizon, just a red background luxuriant with birds and animals and flowers; a circular green sward, abloom with plants; in the middle, a blue pavilion emblazoned with little gold flames or possibly teardrops, bearing a motto— *"mon seul desir."* Before the flaps of the pavilion, held open by a lion and a unicorn, stands a noblewoman dressed resplendently in a red gown. She holds a necklace over a chest carried by a maidservant. A pampered dog is nearby, sitting on a pillow which rests upon a bench. The lion and the unicorn hold banners aloft bearing a coat of arms—a red field with a diagonal blue band and three crescents. A flag with the same device tops the pavilion. Little appears to be happening, yet much is going on.

The pavilion provides a clue to the meaning of the scene, or at least suggests the presence of a unifying theme. Tents are symbols of impermanence; they denote pilgrimage, wandering, even the march of a military campaign. But this tent is securely tied to a holly on one side and a pine on the other, both of which, as evergreens, signify continuity and duration. The theme, therefore, involves change and permanence, or the interpenetration of time and eternity. The crescent in the coat of arms provides another clue. Symbol of so much—a ship, a horn, above all the moon— it too stands for movement, growth, and transformation set within a cycle which itself persists.

Elements of the human drama repeat this theme. In four of the five other tapestries, the noblewoman's hair is beautifully braided or allowed to fall freely down her back below her waist. Here, however, she wears a plumed turban over locks roughly shorn above her shoulders. Since hair is thought to embody energy— with length equated with vitality and strength—it seems as if the woman is abased somehow. Moreover, though long, loose hair on a mature woman can represent freedom and braided hair domestic subjection, cropped hair leaves identity and status undefined. A passage of some sort is suggested, but whether the woman's hair has just been cut or is now growing back—whether she is withdrawing from the world or returning—is left open. In the same way, she stands before an open pavilion, but whether she is coming out or going in is uncertain. Also, in all the other tapestries she wears a necklace, but here her breast is unadorned. She holds a necklace in her hands but whether she has just taken it off and is in the process of putting it away or whether she has just lifted it from the chest and is about to put it on cannot be determined. Like a new or full moon, the woman is perfectly poised between opposing states of being, but not for long—the pendulum will swing, the ceaseless wheel of time will turn, change is certain.

All of this may or may not have something to do with a "sixth sense." If we grant, however, that there is an eternal order behind the flow of time, then perhaps we can say there are moments when our senses are transcended and we experience the world in a different way. We enter a dimension of understanding where past, present, and future coalesce, where words are heard without being spoken, where connections occur with no contact ever made. At this level not only time but space dissolves, for whether we are a thousand miles away from someone or standing side by side, the same pull is felt, the same bond—which is like magnetism or gravity, but stronger. The only force that works like this is love, which may itself be the sixth sense or may at least create the field, beyond the laws of nature, wherein the sixth sense works. For love, in some inscrutable way, draws like to like and fills the world with flowering abundance. It moves the heart, yet keeps it absolutely still.

Whatever the artist's or patron's plan, the whole suite of tapestries, and certainly the sixth one, occasions endless contemplation and projection.

If Edith is imagined as the lady-in-waiting and Una the lady herself, then other elements of the allegory fall into place. The chest that Edith silently raises up between them is filled with memories, the treasures of a lifetime. The chest belongs to Una, for the wealth of the house is hers, but it also belongs to Edith, for she held it in safekeeping. It belongs to both of them, for each gem— each gleaming recollection—is a moment that they shared. The necklace is Edith's book. Crafted of the finest jewels, set to the best of her ability and polished by Edith herself, it captures and reflects the essence of Una's beauty. Una, humbled but still regal, cradles the necklace in her hands. It is wrapped in cloth—too precious, it seems, to touch. While modesty might prevent her from wearing it, longing keeps her from putting it away. So she stands, lost in contemplation, lost in time, knowing that, for as long as she can hold it, what was will forever be.

# Acknowledgments

Even small books have epic histories. Behind this one is Edith Greenan's original impulse to publish her memoir and her wish, in later years, to publish a revised edition. Her wish never materialized, but it was passed on to her daughter Maeve, who listened carefully to the stories her mother told about Robinson and Una, added them to her own vivid memories of life in Carmel, and preserved them with photographs, manuscripts, and other mementos in the family archive. With unselfish and unguarded enthusiasm, with warmth and openness, Maeve shared this archive with me. It was Maeve's devotion to her mother's memory that produced this book.

The devotion of Maeve's brothers, James and Owen, also played a major role. They encouraged Maeve early on, supported her work with me, and then, when the manuscript was finished, carefully read and critiqued it. As writers themselves, they understand that absolute truth is elusive and that point of view determines everything. Though they have their own memories—they, like Maeve, grew up in Carmel and saw everything from the inside—they graciously allowed me to tell their mother's story from my own perspective. I am especially grateful to James Greenan for his insightful advice.

I would like to thank Lee Jeffers for her encouragement and for her willingness to supply photographs. When we looked through her collection together, I was very surprised to find an image of Una and Edith holding *Of Una Jeffers* in manuscript (page 71).

Except for the fact that they are sitting, their pose is remarkably similar to the scene portrayed in the unicorn tapestry, with its hidden associations. I would also like to thank the late Garth Jeffers for his interest in this project at the outset and Brenda Jeffers for providing a photograph. Finally, I would like to express my gratitude to Gil Prince and Robert Zaller for reading and commenting on early drafts of the introduction; Lani and James McManus for providing information about the unicorn tapestry at Cluny; Constance Weissmuller and John Hicks of the Robinson Jeffers Tor House Foundation for steadfast support; and Paula Karman for editorial assistance, loving kindness, and wise counsel throughout.

# OF
# UNA
# JEFFERS

BY
EDITH
GREENAN

THE
WARD RITCHIE
PRESS

*Title page of first edition, 1939*

TO
MY MAEVE,
JIMMY AND OWEN

*For many years I have wished to set down some of my memories of Una and what her friendship has meant to me. This little book grew from that wish. I must express my thanks here to Marcella Burke for her enthusiastic help in giving shape to these memories, and to Robin and Una for their warmest interest, and for permission to print for the first time three poems and a fragment written by Robin.*

E. G.

*This little book characterizes two unusual women and is a memoir of their friendship, but the origin and duration and circumstances of this friendship make it unique I think in literature, and perhaps in life. It began twenty-six years ago; thirty years ago it would hardly have been possible; fifty years ago, hardly conceivable. Even at the present time it would seem an unlikely friendship, yet it has always been natural and unstrained.*

*However, this is not what interested me when I read the book, it was already familiar to me; but the recaptured beauty and simplicity of many incidents and yesterdays moved me rather deeply. There are persons who can savor life fully in its passing moments, as Una Jeffers does, and gather it and savor it again in remembrance. There are others, like myself, to whom things come slowly, and are never quite realized when they happen, but only afterwards, sometimes long afterwards. This little book has made me realize again more fully many lovely memories; and especially the undeserved good fortune that has followed me like a hound, ever since I knew the woman whom Edith Greenan too seems to use for pole-star.*

Robinson Jeffers

*Una at Villa d'Este near Tivoli, Italy,* 1912

I WANTED to meet Una. I wanted to meet her more than anyone else in the world. Una was a wondrous, lovely person. I had heard about her beauty, her brilliance, her understanding. Una had been the wife of the man I was engaged to marry, Edward Kuster. He told me all these things about her. In some curious, indefinable way I began to feel that our marriage would never be a success unless I knew Una.

When Edward first discovered that Una had fallen in love with Robinson Jeffers he couldn't or didn't want to believe what he heard. He didn't even believe Una when she told him honestly and simply, "Yes, it is true, I do love Robin." Edward was stubborn. He asked her to go away, to Europe, for a year, "to think things over." So she had gone, even promised not to write to Robin. After several months a friend wrote, telling her that Edward was interested, absorbed in some other girl. I was that girl!

What Una didn't know was that Edward had already started divorce proceedings. A long time afterwards, when we were close friends, Una told me how overjoyed she was when she heard that "Teddy" had found someone else. It automatically simplified things, it released her. Una was madly in love with Robin, but she had a deep, tender feeling for Teddy. She was very sad. She didn't like hurting him but there was no possible way to avoid it.

On the unforgettable rainy night when Edward took me to meet Una for the first time, I was panic-stricken and pathetically self-conscious. Una was visiting old friends, Hazel and Roy

Pinkham. They lived in a house on a hill, high above Los Angeles. As we rounded the last curve of their driveway I could see the lights of the city below us. I looked at them, silently longing to disappear, to lose myself in that great, impersonal sweep of shimmering light.[1]

We stopped in front of the house and ran quickly up the steps for shelter from the downpour. I remember to this day how I stood there, staring fixedly at the heavy knocker while my knees shook. On the other side of that impressive door was Una![2]

Wild terror seized me. I clung to Edward's arm, speechless. He patted my hand and smiled down at me:

"Don't be frightened, Edith, you two are going to love each other."

I managed a wan sort of smile. Edward lifted the knocker, the door opened, across a charmingly furnished drawing room I saw Una sitting beside an open fire. I recognized her instantly. She was exactly as Edward had described her to me.

When she saw us she rose and walked swiftly across the room. I had never seen anyone so incredibly graceful. Actually Una didn't walk. She smiled, then was there, at our side. She moved without effort, like sunlight.

"Why Edith, how nice!" She leaned over and impulsively kissed me on the cheek. Her deep blue eyes smiled—a warm, friendly greeting.

I was tongue-tied. With a swift, intuitive sense of delicacy she understood my miserable shyness. She didn't wait for me to say anything.

She turned to Edward and with a little exclamation of dismay held out her hands for his driving gloves.[3]

"Gracious, they're soaking wet." She carried them over to the fireplace and placed them on the hearth stones. They were full of rain and quickly made little pools. I thought the gloves standing up from the cuffs looked like desperate hands—raised in supplication.

How illuminating that protective gesture of Una's was. In a flash their former relationship as husband and wife became a formidable barrier. A barrier that had not existed before.

A man says, "my first wife," but those are words making little echoes.

Now, suddenly Una's tenderness, her possessiveness pushed me out of the picture so completely I became more incoherent than I would have been ordinarily. In my heart I knew Una did not do this deliberately to hurt me. She just *hadn't let go of Edward completely.*

Una and Edward had been married for many years. Her concern for his gloves was an unconscious, repetitious little act.

Meeting your husband's *first* wife is far more difficult than meeting his mother. It becomes an emotional, feminine crisis. If Adam and Eve had had to face such undercurrents the human race might have ended then and there.

As the evening passed I watched and listened to Una with a sudden deep emotion. I already adored her. She was the most alluring, unstudied woman I had ever met. I began to hate *me!* I hated being seventeen with such sudden fury it was frightening.

I wondered at the time, too unhappy to see any humor in the occasion, if Una and her friends pitied Edward for his "second choice." I certainly knew they must have been dismayed at my bleak silences. I couldn't talk! I felt lost in Una's rich, intellectual world.[4]

I realized so poignantly the great challenge I had to accept. Una and Edward had shared so much—they *knew* life and the world, they knew and *loved* the arts. I had only a meagre education gleaned from a public school in a small California town. I sensed how preposterous it must have appeared for a young, unsophisticated girl from Bakersfield ever to attempt to take Una's place.

My problem was gargantuan. As all these things passed through my mind I really suffered.

*Portrait of Edith,* c. 1915

Una held the center of the stage the entire evening. The innumerable colorful stories she told filled the room with laughter.[5]

She made a lovely picture wearing a black velvet gown—Empire style—which she herself had designed. Her dark brown hair with red glints in it was bound around her head, making her look more than ever, with her heart-shaped face, like a Botticelli Madonna.[6]

And Una's skin! Unbelievably white, translucent, the texture of jasmine petals.[7] Even her jewelry reflected her individuality. A curious necklace of amber, exquisitely cut. A medieval gold ring and bracelet set with enormous topazes.[8] A delicate, far-away fragrance clung to her. She told me it was sandalwood and that she had never used anything else. I think Una is fond of sandalwood in a mystical sense. It links her with the past, with another very old world she feels at home in. Robin loves it too, and always says by this fragrance he could recognize Una, even in hell.[9]

As we left, I thought perhaps Una harbored a little bitterness, or why had she so completely overshadowed me? But I was wrong. It was inevitable that she should dominate any group of people she was with. And no one ever wants it to be otherwise.

But at the time I confess I had a typical feminine reaction. I felt frustrated by this beautiful woman who was so sure of her every word and gesture. As we drove away I muttered unhappily,

"Edward, that was a Judas kiss of Una's."

"No, Edith, you are wrong," he said. "Didn't you notice, or hear Una humming to herself several times during the evening?"

"Yes, I heard her," I replied gloomily. Edward chuckled, inordinately amused.

"Una was just as nervous over this meeting as you were! She *always* hums when she's nervous!"

Some way, this reassured me. If Una had been self-conscious too, I felt less awkward about our first meeting.

Not long ago Edward and I met at a cocktail party in Hollywood given for Charles Coburn.

Many years had passed since that long-ago night. Edward and I had divorced, and I believe for the first time we had found our rightful places. Edward was now married to a lovely girl called Gabrielle. They had two children.

And I was married to Jim Greenan—and divinely happy. We had three adorable children to make this marriage everything I had dreamed and hoped a marriage would be.

Now, against the background of animated "shop talk" of the theater, pictures, personalities, Edward and I visited for the first time in years. And as always before we talked of Una.

I tried to explain how much her friendship had meant to me, what a beloved figure of guidance she had been.

Edward nodded, understanding perfectly, but he couldn't resist teasing.

"Do you remember how cynical you were? You even suspected Una's kiss!"

I acknowledged this, deeply chagrined.

Edward smiled quizzically, "You know, Edith, I knew I was *right* when I brought you two together. I knew it was *all*, all right, but I was powerless to make it clear to you at that time."

We talked on and on and I was glad of the opportunity it gave me to tell Edward something I had always wanted to say: how truly grateful I was, not alone for Una's friendship which he had made possible, but for the doors he had opened so generously, taking me to my first symphony concerts, to the ballet, to the theater, to see every important artist who came West; for a library of carefully chosen books. "So," I concluded, "you gave me great riches."

"Ah, Edith, you are kind, but Una brought all these things to me first and I, in turn passed them on to you."

We admitted, and no one could know better than we two, Una's great power which moves every life she touches, not alone mine and Edward's and Robinson Jeffers', and her twin boys', Garth and Donnan: everyone is richer for knowing her. And everyone who has been touched by her warm hand has been moulded by it.

Una inherited her passionate Irish nature from her mother.

Her rages and mad bursts of temper are always exciting. There is something forever thrilling about Una's unleashed emotions. And because Robin "is by nature cold," the contrast has never ceased to fascinate him.

"She is more like a woman in a Scotch ballad, passionate, untamed and rather heroic, or like a falcon, than like any ordinary person," writes Robin.

Before they were married occasional letters used to come to Robin from some girl who had, perhaps, fallen in love with him during that time when Una was in Europe. This would make Una simply furious. She resented these letters and the thought of some other woman in Robin's life. She would turn into a thunderbolt of rage and tear the letters into tiny pieces.

"Enough of such things!" she would say, and the air would be full of violent, dire threatenings.

Then Robin would throw his head back and laugh, which is a rare thing for him to do, and he would call her "little savage," and sweep her into his arms and a swift peace would quiet Una's fury. But Robin confesses that he had trembled too.

I asked her one day if her mother ever got as upset about her father as she did about Robin.

"My, yes!" Her eyes twinkled, she quoted the old Gaelic saying,

The women of the village are in madness and trouble,
Pulling their hair and letting it go with the wind.

"Mother behaved exactly like that if my father didn't come home when he was supposed to. She would race up and down the garden with her long hair blowing around her face.

"My father was a sheriff in a small town in Michigan. When he was courting my mother he used to call for her in a sleigh drawn by a pair of beautiful gray horses. Mother was very pretty and quite vain. The first time she went riding with her ardent suitor she wore a long blue chiffon veil. She was terribly proud of it."

Una laughed. "They were riding along ever so gay when all at once the wind tore mother's veil off and it floated away over the snowy field out of sight beyond the black tree tops. Quite a long time afterwards, after mother and father were married, they found wisps of the blue veil woven into a bird's nest in their garden.

"Yeats' mother was very much like mine. He wrote this about her:

She read few books, but she and the fisherman's wife would tell each other stories that Homer might have told, pleased with any moment of sudden intensity, and laughing together over any point of satire. She pretended to nothing she did not feel.

Like her mother Una is delighted with any absurdity, any "abrupt indiscretion of events." It's fun to be with her, so full of gaiety and laughter. Never a shadow across her heart unless someone she loves is in danger. Yet I wonder why her face is often so sad in repose.

One evening, a year after Una and Robin were married, Robin was reading aloud to us. He picked up a book and said, "There is the most perfect description of Una in this. I couldn't have written a better one. De Quincy wrote it, describing Dorothy Wordsworth:

> She was short and slight, a glancing quickness in all her movements, with a warm, even ardent manner and a speech . . . agitated by her excessive organic sensibility. Her eyes not soft but wild and startling which seemed to glow with some subtle fire that burned within her.
>
> The predominant impression was not of the intellect but of the exceeding sympathy, always ready and always profound, by which she made all that one could tell reverberate to one's own feelings by the manifest impression that it made on *hers*. The pulses of light are not more quick or more inevitable in their flow and undulation than were the answering echoes and movements of her sympathizing attention.
>
> I may sum up her character as a companion by saying that she was the very wildest (in the sense of the most natural) person I have ever known, and also the truest, most inevitable, and at the same time the quickest and readiest in her sympathy with either joy or sorrow, laughter or tears, with the realities of life or the eager realities of the poets.
>
> She could sympathize with all the fervor of her passionate heart.
>
> An exquisite regard for common things, a quick discernment of the one point of interest or beauty in the most ordinary incident was the secret of her spell on all who met her.

*Una and Billy,* 1915

The second time I met Una was at the home of Fanny Rowan, a woman of extraordinary charm, friendly and kind toward everyone. "Fan" was a close friend of Una's. They traveled abroad together in 1912. Fanny had just married an Englishman, Harry Young.

Harry and Una had been friends for many years. He had done many pleasant things for Una in England, and he was teasing her about her meeting with a friend of his at a gallery in London. He had said to the man, who had never seen Una, "Look for a Botticelli Madonna wearing a Panama hat." It was Harry who declared years afterwards, when he and Fan and their son were at Tor House, "I don't know whether Una built this tower or wrote the poems. I'll wager she did one or the other."

Robin was at Fan's with Una. It was the first time I had ever seen him.

Fanny was exceedingly gracious. She was one of the few friends who did not seem to mind about Una's divorce.[10] But she was not particularly enthusiastic about Robin! She resented his *not* talking. He was silent the entire evening, just sat and watched Una.[11] She was wearing a soft amber-colored corduroy gown, long waisted, Russian in effect, long full sleeves gathered into tight bands at the wrists—very foreign looking.

Later Fanny said vehemently, "Oh, I could *weep* for Una! If she marries Jeffers it will be a frightful mistake. It can never be a successful marriage!"

Poor Fanny, with her conventional social background, was incapable of coping with such an unsocial person as Robin.

Robin looked then very much as he does today. Tall, lean, rangy, with the greatest restraint in every move he made. Robin doesn't seem to dislike people, or to like them very much. When I talked to him he answered me in a curious low voice. Just a few words, slightly humorous, but to the point.[12]

Robin's eyes are strange, blue-gray in color. It is difficult to look into them, for in some unconscious way his eyes look through and beyond one. When it happens, it is fearsome and disturbing because one feels so *alone* afterwards, so stripped! He seems so distant and *apart* from all of us. But it wasn't an intolerant apartness, never that with Robin. He is too compassionate.

This, my first meeting with Robin, was twenty-six years ago. And it was the second meeting with Una.[13]

I admired her more than ever. With all the fervent adoration a young girl feels for a glamorous older friend. I adored Una and wanted to be like her in every possible way. I even started the next day to design my own clothes, not copying Una's but working out ideas to suit *my* personality; and I went shopping, hoping to find a perfume which would become a part of me, just as Una's sandalwood perfume was identified so unforgettably with her.

Again, Una was the fascinating center of attraction the entire evening. She seemed to be sincerely interested in me and said she hoped I liked her, too, and that we could meet often and become true friends.

Robin and Una went away to live in a cottage by Lake Washington near Seattle. After nine months they returned to stay temporarily with Robin's parents in Pasadena, although Una disliked southern California intensely. She adored the northern hills and sea and wanted to be near them.[14]

She hated the drabness of "just houses" next to each other and across the street from each other. The terrific heat added to her unhappiness. But she liked the big enclosed garden around the Jeffers' home, filled with flowers and every kind of fruit. "We are leading a Theocritan life here," she wrote me, "sitting under the grape arbor through the hot shimmering afternoons, the air heavy with fragrance of peaches and roses. Later the nice man who lives next door will come along that marigold path to bring me a yellow bowl brimming with goat's milk." She was happy with the simplicity of life in the Jeffers family. The music, the books and the walks in the evenings. Una, at this time, had no desire for parties or people. She only wanted to have Robin with her. She was in the first ecstasy of love fulfilled and looking forward to a radiant future. Her days began and ended with Robin.

She called Robin's mother "Belle-mère." Mrs. Jeffers was a tall woman who carried herself proudly erect at all times. She had great dignity and grace, great refinement, and an interesting cultural background. Her forbears were Tuttles and Robinsons who played an important rôle in New England. An accomplished musician, she sang and played the piano and organ exceptionally well. It was she who said after Una and Robin married, that it was Una and Una alone who could bring her son to great accomplishments.[15]

I never saw Robin's father but I have heard many stories about his brilliant scholastic record. I felt as though I knew him much better after going into his library. He was a distinguished theologian, a scholar in Latin, Greek, Hebrew and Arabic. He had travelled extensively in Syria, Greece and Egypt. He was many years older than Robin's mother. He died in December in the year 1914. Before that, when I had been at the Jeffers' home, Una had invariably said, "The Doctor is put away in his library deciphering something very erudite!" With all her love of scholarship she fainted at mention of Sanscrit and Hebrew.

Una has given me permission to print this hitherto unpublished poem of Robin's. It is one of the many morning songs he wrote to her. Each day when she opened her eyes, there beside her was a poem or a little freshly gathered nosegay. This one was written in Pasadena in 1915. They slept there on a balcony which overhung the garden; yellow and white Banksia roses cascaded over it, mockingbirds sang all night in the pepper trees beside it, and little wandering winds brought them fragrance from dew-drenched flowers—all a part of that Theocritan idyl.

TO U. J.

Come with me into my vineyard,
O sister, O my bride,
While tenderest light is being drawn
As with well-buckets from the morning side
To make the sky a lake filled full of day;
For liquid is the light and tenderest gray
This rainy dawn.

Come, we will walk in our vineyard.
There is no rain, what did I say of rain?
Except, it rained all night feeding the flowers.
And if you were awake you must have heard
That Lesbian-throated mockingbird
Moulding such music between showers
As only lovers ought to listen to.
And l was right to listen, and would fain
Have wakened you,
Love, love! to listen. When the rainfall stopped,
How chokingly, how passionately abrupt,
What bursts of gold, that song! A golden chain,
Notes linked by love's fulfilment; our love too
Complete; and in the night rejoiced
The whole flaming soul of spring, perfectly voiced.

Come walk with me in the vineyard,
The odors are all so sweet,
The leaves are long already and broad,
The grapes in clusters hung
Are still so young, so young,
Like little green grains of wheat;
Yet they are full of a God,
And he so young, so young!

Hung wide over our vineyard,
O sister, O my bride,
Is not this tenderest gray sky of light
Just colored like the under side
Of one of the leaves of the long vine?
And on the skyward face of every leaf
The gemmed and clustered raindrops shine
Tenderly bright:
Pearls, would you say?
Ah brief and delicate delight!
Catch it, for it is brief;
And never another morning of any year

Will be like this one, O most dear;
Never such tenderness and beauty allied,
Never such fragrance, never a gray so gay,
O my heart's twin sister, sister and bride,
Not till the years of time are fled away,
Not till our loves are dead and deified.

We have met three Gods in our vineyard
Up at the hill's brow.
Iacchus is one and Love is one,
There is a greater still
Here on the brow of the hill.
And when, under what sun
In the world, or how,
In what extreme day
Golden or gray,
Have ever another poet and his bride
Gone hand in hand, side by side,
Talking of wonderful gifts and signs,
Walking with Gods between vines. . .
O full of Gods is the vineyard,
And I am silent now.

SPRING, 1915
PASADENA

I felt so immature and such a great distance behind these wonderful new friends. It used to seem to me as though they had read and heard and done everything. There was an incredible amount of ground to be covered if I ever hoped to catch up with them. I tried to give them an idea of my childhood, of those vivid, lawless days which had helped to make history in California.

I came from the Kern County town when it was still *"Wild West!"* The hills were filled with desperadoes. Those same mountain passes of ledged caves and scrub oaks in clustered entanglements that Stevenson said murderers might hide in.

I can remember vividly the Sunday night that Kinney, the bandit, rode into Bakersfield and killed the sheriff and his two deputies, including Bert Tibbett, father of the now famous Lawrence Tibbett, the singer.

It was an excessively hot Sunday afternoon. I was all dressed up in my best dress, walking toward the village for my great weekly treat, an ice cream soda! My father's secretary rushed out, grabbed hold of me and turned me back in the direction of our house. She screamed at me to go home, there was shooting going on at that very moment. I could hear it and I was suddenly terrified as was everyone else. The women had pulled all the curtains down at their windows, only the braver ones dared to peek out. For hours everyone stayed at home, barricading themselves in with anything they could put their hands on. Mother pulled me in the front door so quickly my feet didn't even touch the floor. She was panic-stricken.

But they finally cornered Kinney down in the red-light district, which was about the largest part of Bakersfield in those days. Kinney was hiding down there but someone recognized him and they shot it out to the finish.

They carried his body into the drugstore where we got our ice cream sodas. It was one of those funny old-fashioned drug stores with the big green and red globes of water in the windows. Souvenir hunters snitched bits of Kinney's clothing while he lay there in a sort of unholy state. He was there for display purposes, not for interment.[16]

In 1915 Hazel Pinkham got me interested in going to the Denishawn school of dancing. A superficial group of society women frequented the classes, hoping to make their figures beautiful.

I must confess I started out with the same idea. After the first lesson, dancing became an obsession with me. Ted Shawn and Ruth St. Denis became interested in my work. I took private lessons from Ruth. She used to create during these private lessons, special interpretative studies which I have never forgotten. As she would create the movements, I would follow step by step. I soon lost myself completely under her hypnotic force.

One day after I had finished a terrifically difficult dance, Ruth called over "Brother" St. Denis, her stage manager. She made me dance again for him. Afterwards she said, "Remember, Brother, I found this girl and she's going to make a great artist. She is my 'nut-brown maid'!"

Those days of intensive hard work and practicing and study were memorable ones. Ruth St. Denis was incomparable. Her teachings, given from her very soul, inspired many of my young friends who were pioneers in the Denishawn School. Martha Graham and the lovely little Mary Hay, Ada Forman, Betty Horst, Ruth Austin, Doris Humphrey, Margaret Loomis, Florence Andrews.[17]

Curiously enough, Una did not share my enthusiasm for interpretative dancing. I think now, as I look back, her lack of interest was entirely due to the fact that she was only interested in making a new home for Robin. And she wanted children! Nothing else mattered. To her, a career for a woman was a meaningless thing. I am convinced that *had* Una encouraged me during that particular phase of my life, I undoubtedly would have made every sacrifice necessary to become a great dancer.

Subconsciously, I was very aware of a completeness in Una's life which I lacked. Sadly enough, my marriage with Edward was not the solution. From the very beginning, in those early days of Una's marriage to Robin, we couldn't help but feel alone and insignificant in contrast to their all-absorbing passion for each other. There has never been a love like theirs!

If Una suspected that our marriage was doomed to be a failure, never by a word or sign did she intimate such a possibility. On the contrary, she gave me invaluable advice. Advice founded in an understanding of Edward which I never achieved.[18]

*Edith in Dance Costume*, c. 1918

During the months they waited for the birth of their first child Una and Robin lived in La Jolla in a little house called "Breezy Nest." It was perched high upon a hill above the sea. We used to visit them there and had great fun walking over the rocks and cliffs. La Jolla in those days had not been invaded by realtors. It was an untouched little village.

We had some jolly, silly jaunts together; one was to the San Diego Fair in 1915.[19] I remember Robin attempted to ride a fast revolving plate but he was projected off into space with the rest of us. "Try to be dignified and slow there, my lad," Una jibed at him. We stopped to eat our supper on the seashore by Laguna, a lovely remote spot in those days. Darkness fell, and I planted four

*Teddie, Edith, and Robinson* (Photographed by Una), c. 1915

candles in the sand for light—four bits of flame that remained steadfast against the night, when we looked back as we drove slowly along the cliffs. This is one of the little glowing memories put carefully away in my mind—and in theirs too, for Robin made a little poem about it.[20]

One night at San Gabriel I saw a frightened Una. My (once *her*) brindle bulldog, Beau Brummel, was famous for the lightning speed of his movements. The cook had discovered a family of mice living in a disused flour-bin, and we watched the hunt. In dived Beau, swallowed several, and emerged with flour all over his crazy wrinkled face. He dashed toward Una, one mouse still clutched in his teeth. Una leaped onto a chair and shrieked. It was very comical, flour everywhere, and Beau feverishly determined to win her applause. Robin and all of us—except Una—shouted with laughter.

Perhaps it is only mice she fears, for since then I've seen her accept some very curious pets. Besides the lovebirds and ring-doves and bantams there have been a fierce hawk with broken wing, a baby bat named Noctule and fed with an eye-dropper, two repulsive snakes that Lady Hastings gave the boys. Una did rebel at guinea pigs with their possibilities.[21]

Robin was a magnificent swimmer and used to go in the sea every day. Una and Billy, their English bull, stood watch on the cliff. Meanwhile Robin, completely oblivious of time or distance, would swim out so far Una couldn't even see his head. Then she would go mad with fear. When Robin reappeared, she scolded and wept and laughed through her tears of relief. She was always terrified, yet fascinated by his prowess, battling through those winter waves.

Never were two lives any happier. The days flew past, one more joyous than the last. Una sewed, she made exquisite little garments for her baby whom she always called "Donnan." When the time came for her confinement, Robin brought Una back to Los Angeles so that her friend, the famous obstetrician, Dr. Titian Coffey, could deliver the child.

A beautiful little girl was born whom Una immediately named Maeve, out of an Irish legend. Two days later the child died. The shock almost killed Una, she was inconsolable. Delirious for days, she kept repeating over and over again so piteously, "I want my baby, I want my baby." I didn't see the baby afterwards, I was too shattered; but Hazel Pinkham said they used the net and lace carriage cover which I had made, for an ephemeral little shroud. It was a heartbreaking tragedy to survive, but Una was very brave. She said to me with rare tears pouring down her face, "I will not look back. One has to learn to close doors."[22]

It was after this that Una and Robin came to Carmel to live. Frederick Mortimer Clapp, one of Una's dearest friends in the world, knew and loved Carmel. He had described many times its unforgettable beauty.

So they came north to explore, to find out for themselves if they should make their home there. They fell in love with it from the moment they came over the hill from Monterey. They searched for a house and found a log cabin built on the edge of a canyon, close to the sand dunes and the sea.

Una wrote me ecstatic letters and invited me up for a visit. Of course I accepted, I couldn't get there fast enough.[23]

Una and Robin met me at the train in Monterey. I peered eagerly out of the window and saw that beautiful bay filled with little blue Spanish and Italian fishing boats. Fish nets were draped haphazardly over the fields—they seemed even to cover the funny little Chinese laundries near the water front.

Robin picked up my bags and put them underneath the seat of the surrey Una was driving. We got in and started gaily away in the direction of Carmel.

I marvelled at Una—she handled those two spirited horses so expertly. I've always been terrified of horses, of being on their backs or behind their tails. As we rode along, my terror grew by leaps and bounds. Una was so unconcerned. She chattered away, pointing out fascinating old adobe houses. She gave new luster to everything she spoke about. I felt as though I were riding in a Juggernaut, riding head on into inevitable annihilation. There was one little street car track in Monterey. My fear was great that Una would get the wheels of our buggy caught in that track. I no sooner thought of this, than it happened.

Undisturbed, Una sat up straighter than ever, completely disregarding the fact that she had done anything awkward. She refused to admit, by the turn of a hair, that a mild catastrophe had occurred. Miraculously, or so it seemed to be, she extricated us. The wrenched wheel revolved like a disgruntled egg beater, making a hideous sound. Of course people turned and laughed at our ridiculous progress up the street. Robin sat beside Una, not saying a word. He didn't mention the accident, and I didn't dare to.

As we drove up the steep grade toward Carmel, Una stopped to let the horses rest and to point out to me the Monterey Bay behind us—a perfect, blue crescent, one of the most beautiful bays in the world. To the east of it, behind a black line of pine trees, is Del Monte.

A few minutes later we started down Ocean Avenue, the steep dirt road into Carmel. In those days there were only a few stores on the main street. No one seemed to be greatly concerned with business. Many times we've gone to a store only to find it closed and a sign in the door, "Back in two hours." "Pop" Slevin ran the stationery store combined with a makeshift post office. It was the meeting place extraordinary.

When we reached Carmel, we got out and left the horses at Hodges', then Gould's, Livery Stable. We walked the rest of the way—down a joyous little path to the log cabin. It was very early, one of those exciting spring mornings when the entire world seemed to be turning cartwheels over the hills, down to the sea. All of Carmel was lost beneath a cloud of wild lilac and the air filled with its fragrance.

The road to the cabin dwindled away to nothing; we were remote from human kind. But, "No," Una said, "there are people near by, hidden in the forest. Listen what happened yesterday. Robin was chopping wood by the back door and motioned me to come out. A voice was ringing through the trees, a woman's voice, loud and threatening: 'Blood. . . savagery rampant. . . shoot them down. . . .' We were astounded and delighted by this outburst. Then we discovered in the village 'twas Mary Austin practicing a speech she means to deliver at an anti-war meeting in Golden Gate Park. Her cottage is across this gulch."

That log cabin era is one of my most beautiful memories. The cabin was not large, a living room with an enormous fireplace, one bedroom and bath and an excessively small kitchen.[24]

Una cooked all the meals on an old iron stove. She did it so gaily. But it made me uneasy to see her struggling with the fire and lifting the heavy iron lids. When I went back to Los Angeles I sent her up a two-burner oil stove which she said simplified things remarkably.[25]

By the fireplace was one of those big brown baskets used by Chinamen to carry fish, kelp and vegetables. Una had found it on the shore. It was always filled with driftwood, choice bits kept for their grotesque shapes, twisted bone-white likenesses of beasts and birds, or frayed oak planks showing certain dark stains where copper and brass nails had once held fixtures of metal. These pieces were certain to burn with brilliant flaming greens, blues and orange when Una carefully laid them upon the coals, murmuring, "'Is all our fire of shipwreck wood, oak and pine?' Well, as James Lee's wife says, 'Hell beneath!'" Browning was another of her favorites then.

Above the fireplace was a wide shelf and upon it a small stone cross she had brought back from Cornwall, a jug of wild flowers, fragrant yellow clover—"melilot" she liked to call it—and irises if Una could get them, particularly the very pale blue ones which grew only in one patch, on the slope where the gate now opens to Palo Corona Ranch. There was also a small mirror set into a wooden frame, crudely carved but worn very smooth, with a wooden cover swinging on a wooden hinge over its face. They had found this hanging to a tree near by and supposed it must belong to the log cabin, so left it there when they departed. Afterwards the woman who owned the house thanked Una for this wonderful relic, a museum piece from the old Spanish days. They never found out its history. Oh how Una wished she'd kept it!

One night we sat by the fire listening to the high wind which sounded like sea waves through the trees close against the house. Robin begged Una to read Synge's *Riders to the Sea*. Her low voice rising and falling brought into the room the beat of the sea and the relentless surge of grief; tears streamed from her eyes with Maurya's final words about her drowned sons: "Bartley will have a fine coffin out of the white boards, and a deep grave surely. . . . No man at all can be living forever, and we must be satisfied."[26]

While we sat there still shaken, there came a broken tapping. "Oh Robin, it is a white bird the wind has dashed against the pane!" Her pale face was whiter still. Robin opened the window, reached out a great hand and gently enclosed the little creature. "It *isn't* white after all, it's someone's little lost canary," and she carried it into the kitchen to spend the night perched on the towel-line. "What if it *had* been white?" I wondered. Then Una, still under the Gaelic spell, was telling us an old tale of white birds coming out of the night as omens of Death.[27] Years after, she read me this refrain rescued from an unpublished poem of Robin's:

> Fleet birds go flying
> Through the wind over the sea,
> Birds of the dying
> On wings unheard.
> Foremost that old man's bird
> Beautiful among three,
> A white bird and two red,
> Gray rain over the sea,
> Souls of three people dead,
> Dear souls to me,
> Go flying, go vanishing, flying.

Una told us she once had another curious experience of a bird coming out of the night. It was when she and Edward Kuster were living in Los Angeles. He called to her from the garden back of the house—it was late twilight, there in the path stood a wild duck. How came it there alone and alien in the midst of a crowded city?

Una had been much under the spell of Ibsen's *Wild Duck*, and sensed in this some mysterious symbol or omen. They watched the creature until it rose silently, and without circling, winged a direct course away north—on what far flight?

As soon as we finished breakfast in the morning, we went for a walk down the canyon, then on a trail which wound through the forest. There were wildflowers running helter-skelter—everyplace —so many unfamiliar ones I had never seen before. But Una knew all their names. She pointed out triumphantly the fairy lanterns and the sticky monkey plant and the lovely Indian paint brush. Once she dashed away from the path and called out over her shoulder, "Robin, here is a perfectly precious little wild rose!"

Finding a wild rose was exciting, especially the year's first one.

Suddenly at the end of a trail we came out upon the white strange sand dunes, close to the sea. Una always ended her walks along this eerie white stretch of sand. Robin called her "Little Seaward." After my first visit, Una wrote me, "Robin now calls you 'Little Seaward the Second.'"

Sometimes sunset would find us by the water-meadow near the river-mouth. Clouds of gulls rose up and circled away to the north to their secret resting place. We would lean against the old rail fence and watch the rose light fade from the pools, and creeping shadows blot out the farther hills, then the nearer ones, then the trees and the farmhouse. "Look," Una said, "that's exactly what Meredith saw—'Darker grows the valley, more and more forgetting. . . .'"

Those daily expeditions were always eventful, for Una didn't *just* walk. She was so aware, so conscious of all the beauty around us. She taught me to *see*, and how to use my eyes! Occasionally Robin and Billy would dash away to some distant knoll and with a furious abandon would go leaping down to the edge of the sea. This never failed to delight Una. She loved watching great, tall Robin racing down the steep sand dunes, and Billy off and away

*Edith, Una, and Billy,* 1919

*Robinson, Una, and Billy,* 1919

to scare up flocks of sea gulls from the sand. She called him "old General Twinklefoot"; he was lame in one front foot and had such a funny gait when he ran.[28]

When we went for longer walks in the hills I was amazed to discover Una's familiarity with every inch of that wild country. She not only knew the names of all the wild flowers, but the names of all the birds and the trees! She revelled in the mysterious, brooding beauty of the Santa Lucia Mountains. In those early days the Big Sur district down the coast was practically inaccessible. The first time Robin and Una had gone down, they drove the dangerous sea road with horses and wagon.[29]

It was during one of these early trips that they came upon the ranch house built of squared redwood logs which Robin used later for a scene in one of his first great poems.

Una has a great gift. She can be alone with a stranger for two seconds or five minutes and come away with a fragment of some incredible story. It was Una who talked with an old resident of the Big Sur. He told her the last owner of the abandoned ranch house had been killed by his stallion. And out of this Robin conceived *Roan Stallion.*

From the very beginning Una gathered up the eerie tales around and about the strange Santa Lucia Mountains—from the secret caves and landing places along the shore, from farmers, from fishermen, from all kinds of people. Una has such a glorious way of coming back home and telling some small incident, dramatizing, building an entire legend out of it.[30]

Robin and Una were intensely interested in the stars. They were studying star-charts, and every night we watched the constellations wheel across the sky. There was talk of evening and morning stars, and the colors of Sirius and red Antares. They pointed out the line of the zodiac, with sighs of grief from Una that it was hopeless for them to try to tell the hour of the night by a glance at the sky, as Gabriel Oak did. Una would smile a bit shyly after these talks and say, "Of course Robin's brother Hamilton is a real astronomer. He is very embarrassed about what color

Aldebaran seems to me. He talks in terms of meridian circles and orbits of comets!"

Point Lobos is one of Una's favorite haunts.[31] With the fog swirling around, it made me think of the scene from *Tristan and Isolde* when Tristan is dying. You can hear the shepherds' pipes playing off somewhere among the trees.

When we used to drive out for a picnic on Point Lobos the horses would invariably rear and plunge, refusing to go under the gnarled old cypress trees. There is something so sinister and frightening about the place. One hears that years ago, Indians used to have human sacrifices on Lobos. Lobos is the scene of Robin's *Tamar.*

I liked to swim in the sea at the mouth of the Carmel River. Una and Robin would stand by and watch me. Robin never swims in Carmel Bay. He says the water there comes straight from the Arctic Ocean. When Robin took the twins in one day a sudden mask of fear came over Una's face. She told me afterwards, in her horoscope there is a notation of danger by water. But somehow she must have conquered this fear later, or defied it, for after Robin taught the boys to swim in the river-mouth they went into the rough sea every day; people would gather along the road to see the waves throw them among and over the jutting rocks below, and they as indifferent as seals. And Robin tells me that not long ago Una went down to the little cove every day for over a year in sun and rain and wind for a morning dip. But at that time I alone went in.

When I played around in the surf I felt like a dancer in the great robe of the elements, with the wind and the waves and the tide. Robin said, "Edith, you skim the water like some beautiful sea bird. I shall never go to the shore again without seeing a bacchante along the edge of the foam." I recalled those moments with great joy when I re-read Robin's lyric, "Fauna." Una said I had helped Robin to the vision of Fauna, dancing ankle-deep, in the lapping waves.

Every day was such a perfect blending of the practical things

*Edith Dancing on Seashore, I*

*Edith Dancing on Seashore, II*

that had to be done and the things that were beautiful. There was no outside social life in those early Carmel days. We always went down to the beach and hoisted driftwood onto our shoulders to carry home for the fires.

Una invariably stopped right in the midst of cooking to tell Robin and me some fascinating thing. Or she would look out of the window—then, enraptured by the flash of a blue-jay's wing or the beauty of the pine trees, she would bring that beauty into the room and give it to us—rare gifts, given so lavishly, so exquisitely.[32]

The food Una prepared was always substantial. For breakfast, huge bowls of well-cooked oatmeal with rich yellow cream. Delicious coffee. Luncheon was simple—thick slices of wonderful warm bread, cheese and milk and wild flower honey we had fetched from the honey man. Dinner was the important meal of the day. If we had meat or fish it meant a trip to Monterey. All was served "on the bare boards"; the table was a cross section of the trunk of a great sugar pine; the surface slanted but was scrubbed smooth and snow white.

In contrast to my instinctive extravagances Una's frugality never ceased to intrigue me. She would get so cross if anything went to waste. To her wastefulness was a sin—too stupid to be endured. She made an art of economy.[33]

Economy or moderation of any sort were unknown traits to a native-born Californian. We grew up throwing away our possessions with a prodigal hand to the four winds, never doubting for one moment but that the four winds would replenish us in due time.

One night I committed an unforgivable sin. In clearing away the dishes I thoughtlessly threw a rind of cheese into the fire. The next day Una was busily preparing some macaroni for our dinner. She began to open and shut the cupboard doors, frantically searching for something. Exasperated, she turned and said, "*Edith*, did you or Robin do anything with that piece of cheese that was left last night?"

I glanced at Robin apprehensively. I could tell by the subdued laughter in his eyes that he was aware of my guilt. I trembled, I longed for the floor to open up so that I could disappear just long enough to return with a new piece of cheese.

Una stood before me, waiting for an answer.

I managed after two attempts to tell her I had thrown it away and how sorry I was.

"Never mind, we'll just have to have the macaroni without cheese," she said sternly. "It's too bad because there was just enough left to make it perfectly delicious."

Even now I watch them at Tor House gather up with almost superstitious care all discarded crumbs to spread in the courtyard for the birds.

It used to be such fun to watch Una out on the fishermen's wharf at Monterey. She would stand and wait most patiently while the men started to unload their catches. As the net, brimful of silver fish, would swing up from the boat and down onto the wharf, Una would see the *exact* fish she wanted and dart over and grab hold of its tail and hang on to it until one of the laughing fishermen would disentangle it for her.

Then she would bargain for it. Una knew *exactly* how much a fish should cost. She might concede the fact that a salmon cost a trifle more than some fat sea bass, but they couldn't and didn't dream of overcharging her. After this we would drive out to some nearby ranch and get fresh berries and eggs, then home and Una would cook the fish or the pot roast superbly.

But there was invariably one most important place to stop before we left Monterey—the old adobe wine shop! The Italian and his wife who owned the place used to sprinkle the bare, unpainted floor with water to keep it cool. Robin would take a huge, wicker-covered demijohn inside and get it filled with Angelica wine. No one drank before dinner, always afterwards! After the dishes were washed, Una or Robin would fill great tumblers with the wine and we would sit by the fire and sip it while Robin read aloud to us.

He always read Shelley in those days, and occasionally Swinburne or even Maeterlinck. Una gave me many books to read, the ones she loved most. There were Yeats and Moore, Arthur Symons, Pater, the Brontës, Dostoevski and Hardy, and d'Annunzio's *The Flame of Life*.[34] And innumerable volumes of Irish legends. Una turned to me one day with a well-thumbed copy of Wordsworth in her hands and said, "Poetry, Edith, bears great fruit for living. Poetry is first, last, and all the time, for in it you will find something that is nowhere else in literature." She confided to me with a grin that her high school graduating oration had been entitled "The Poet." "It was very flowery—I looked quite sweet and enthusiastic when I delivered it—wish Robin had seen me!"[35]

The following year Una was again expecting the arrival of another child.[36] Again they made a trip south, so that Dr. Coffey could officiate. Instead of one child, Una produced twin boys, Garth and Donnan. Una told me afterwards that they came so fast she didn't have an anesthetic. The doctor said, "Here is *son*, Una."

She laughed when she spoke of this incident. "I sank back, thrilled to death—at last I had a son. But no sooner did I start to relax when Dr. Coffey said, 'Here is another boy!' There was no doubt about it, for he showed it to me, and so I was forced to believe him. Then he began to be very efficient once again. To tease me, when the afterbirth came he said, 'Una! Triplets!' That was too much to endure. I sat halfway up on the delivery table and roared at him, 'There couldn't be a third!' He and all the nurses laughed at my indignant protest. But I was never so happy in all my life as when I realized I had given birth to twin boys!"

Of course no visitors were permitted to see Una for a week. When I finally tiptoed into that hospital room she looked more like a Madonna than ever, with her long braids outside the white spread. Robin, great tall Robin, was standing by the bed, staring down at his two lively, lusty sons. There was an expression of in-

*Una with Twins and Billy*

credulous wonder and worship on his face as he watched Una's radiance. He called her "little apple blossom."

When she was permitted to leave the hospital Robin took his little family over to his mother's home in Pasadena. The day I went to see them there, Robin greeted me in the hallway, "Have you come to see the feast? They're upstairs."

I went up into Una's room. She had just finished bathing and rubbing the twins with oil. She looked pale with dark circles under her eyes. It worried me. I wondered if she had the necessary strength to undertake all of these duties besides nursing her infant sons.[37]

But Una's fierce love was a possessive one. She wanted to do everything for her babies herself. She scoffed at the idea of a nurse. Her greatest joy in life was to be with her two sons and with Robin.

Una wrote me a letter long afterwards when she was back in Carmel and I was south:

*Edith and Una with
Garth and Donnan*

"I nursed the twins for ten months and apparently I'm the only woman in history who ever did."

The little Jeffers family came back to Carmel-by-the-Sea and moved out of the log cabin into a larger, sunnier house. This second house was a brown shingled bungalow, the Tretheway house, later owned by Tom Cator, a typical Carmel house panelled inside with redwood. They lived there for more than two years. I visited them often in this house—the days were very busy and planned around the twins' schedule.

After the babies were safely tucked away we would drink our coffee by the fire. Later the big wicker-cased demijohn of wine was brought out, and Robin read to us. Una was making the little smocks that the boys wore for several years—they were always of the same amber-colored linen, a single brown butterfly embroidered on Garth's, a swallow on Donnan's. Sometimes Una and Robin asked me to dance and I would improvise, either to interpret a mood or simply variations of rhythmical themes based on Mrs. Hovey's methods. Una thought these very beautiful: I remember one morning she wrote down copious notes and said, "Now if I can just get the boys raised, I am going to do these and be very beautiful, too!"

There came a day when two of my friends from Hawaii arrived to see "Edith's matchless Carmel"; one was Edith Williams (called *Kulumanu*) of the Castle family long important in Island affairs, sister of the beautiful and fabulous Claire Cartwright. The other was Abie Buchanan, in whose veins flowed a rich strain of royal Hawaiian blood. She was fascinating and exotic. A mysterious cloud hung over her, for an island girl had put a curse on her after Abie had won some native prize for dancing. Her health had become frail and she did in fact die young, a few years later. One evening we went to the Jeffers' house carrying hula skirts and various lovely colored scarves and chiffons. There was a long living room with a corner windowseat at one end. The moon was full that night. It filled those windows, and in its glow sat Una, gay and vibrant in a brilliant flame-colored sari I had wrapped round her, and Robin with a lei of ferns—we insisted that everyone must be festive at a native dance. Already we had filled the room with flowers and green branches.

The Hawaiian dances fascinated me and I had worked hard to learn the hula and some of the ritualistic movements of the ceremonial dances from Kulumanu, whom I first met at Denishawn. We danced before our friends to the music of our Hawaiian phonograph records. Una clapped her hands with the beat of the drums and was completely delighted with the suppleness of Abie's lovely body when she bent backward to pick a scarf from the ground with her teeth. We grew more and more excited as the evening wore on—it was only when very late—very early in the morning

—wails began to come from the twins' room—that we piled hula skirts and the other props in a corner and slipped away through the forest shadows to our cabin.

Later Una and Robin bought a beautiful piece of property out on the Point with the sea beneath them and Point Lobos forever a part of their new world.

When they were building their house out on the Point, Robin planted two thousand eucalyptus and cypress trees. Of them he writes,

> And beyond them the jets of young trees
> I planted the year of the Versailles peace.

Today the branches meet overhead, as you walk the back path to the house, like an arch of drawn sabres at an army wedding.

A builder in Carmel called Murphy built the first part of the Jeffers house. His wife had had twins, so she loaned Una her twin baby buggy.

I came up more and more often to visit Una in Tor House. I

*Tor House,* 1919

*Living Room of Tor House* by Morley Baer

would bring a few little gifts with me. It was such fun to see Una's delight over the simplest thing. She has tiny feet, size two. It was difficult for her to get grown-up shoes that small, so she compromised and wore little girl patent leather slippers, the kind Alice in Wonderland always wore.

Una admired the sandals I wore when I was studying at Denishawn, so to surprise her I had some made—little white leather ones. I think she liked those more than any other gift I ever gave her.

People invariably *give* Una things. She is so generous with herself, so outgoing in her warmth when she is a friend, one has a desire to make her happy. And since Una has such definite hobbies, it is so easy to search for the thing you know she will adore.

Unicorns and George Moore, garnets and aquamarines, honey and asphodel bulbs from Hymettus, sandalwood perfume, Fortuny gowns, Jugtown pottery, Irish whiskey, melodeons and Gaelic music. I'm sure if you should bring Una the right songs from the heart of Ireland you would forever win a place in *her* heart. And books! And rocks! Rocks from the graves of poets, or from the round towers of Ireland, even a stone from Croagh Patrick, a holy mountain in County Mayo, or the Temple of Heaven in China. Any rock, sacred for some memory, Una loves, because Robin builds them into her tower, and she has great fun pointing them out to visitors and telling strange stories to match their origin.

Oh yes, Una loves madonnas, and has the most beautiful one in a specially built niche in her little tower room. She is Spanish and very old, dressed in ancient brocades of maroon and black. Her face is made of delicately colored wax, her eyes of glass. What poignant sadness and gentle dignity in that little figure! Over the niche printed in gold letters on the stone is "Madonna de la Torre," and at her feet a medal Una found in the Cathedral in Milan and a rosary, a poor little rosary Una picked up at the foot of the Round Tower in Kells, Ireland.

In humorous contrast to so many of the fragile, beautiful things Una loves, are epitaphs—and Billy, their ugly, handsome English bull. But the story about Billy's death comes later.

Every morning at Tor House started exactly the same way. Una never once deviated from her daily ritual. Very early she would jump out of bed and light the air-tight heater to make the room warm up quickly for the twins. Then Una would take a cold bath! For some reason she thought this was an important thing to do. She would roar like a lion all the time she was taking it. I used to wake up in my room and start laughing at her self-torture. The next move was to get a huge bowl of corn flakes and milk and three spoons, and Una's voice saying, "One for Garth, one for Donnan, and *one* for mother,"—this kept up until the corn flakes were all gone.

Meanwhile Robin made the coffee. After this, the twins' bath!

That was a tumultuous event. After this Una would make Robin's breakfast. When breakfast was finished the twins were put outside in a little pen to play while Una made the beds, swept, washed the breakfast dishes and several times a week washed the clothes for the family. I happened to be there on a visit when Dr. Coffey came up from Los Angeles to see how the twins were doing. He said, "They're too white, Una."

Instantly Una was panic-stricken, hurtling questions at Dr. Coffey about what should be done.

He said, "Scraped beef and spinach put through a sieve!" This meant extra tedious work but of course Una did it, and did it most expertly.

Young Donnan wouldn't eat his; he would just hold the food in his mouth, disdaining another spoonful. Una grew more and more frantic. One day when she was worn out, she suddenly lost her temper. She screamed at Donnan, "Eat your food!" Robin made one start across the room, then stopped. He realized it was her problem and it was best to let her cope with it alone. He just came and stood by poor Una.

She spanked Donnan and Garth cried because Donnan was howling. Then they both got sick and lost their food and Una wept bitterly. But that was the last time Donnan refused to swallow his spinach and scraped beef.

I used to marvel at Una's endless activities; they were simply overwhelming. She made the boys' moccasins by hand—God knows how many dozens of pairs. And she made their clothes and Robin's shirts! As they commenced to wear out, she mended and darned them. And broken sleep at night, jumping up two or three times to take the twins to the bathroom.

And the wondrous thing about it all was Una's joy in doing these things. At night when the boys were asleep, Una would sit by the fire and unbraid her beautiful hair and brush it while Robin read aloud. Suddenly, she looked like a little girl—wistful, adorably appealing. . . sitting there with tiny bare feet.

*Robinson and Una with Twins, c. 1920*

Una said so many thrilling things happened all the time, she hated to go away from home, for a day even. She spoke of the great meteor that made an arc of flaming green and blue over Tor House into the sea; the ship loaded with a cargo of paper that they watched burning from dawn to midnight, drifting along the horizon off Carmel Bay; the mysterious lights that flashed from rocks and sea during the days of prohibition smuggling. And there was a car that dashed over the cliff late one night: it landed upside down, broken and twisted, but its lights still burned. Una and Robin ran down to help. Its occupant had vanished, only a desperate-looking shoe stuck out from underneath, "but no foot in it," she adds earnestly. And they have had many queer visitors, by day and by night, with odd requests. One day Una saw a pretty, elfish girl in the courtyard, bending over the rosemary bush. "Perhaps you didn't know," the girl explained with a strong Highland Scotch accent, "I own a bit of this land here, for I slid in one day last summer and buried a crooked sixpence." One of the most exciting episodes was when they watched a midnight meeting of the

Ku Klux Klan near the standing stone at the north boundary of Tor House property, just where it joins Kuster's land. White-robed figures moved ceremoniously and burned a fiery cross. Una chuckled through the binoculars, watching the initiates bow to their leader. The Rosicrucian order is said to have owned the land about that stone long ago, and perhaps lifted there at certain times their *Rosy* Cross, the ancient symbol of their order.

And there have always been exciting observations of birds—once an incredible flock of shearwaters streamed past like a black flood all of one day. Again there was the beauty of sun flashing on the snowy wings of twenty-one wild swans early one morning. Una reported, "Andrew Stewart says *thousands* of wild swans flew over in the old days. They would often alight in the water meadow—or even come into the barnyard to pick up grain." Even yesterday Una and Robin saw a white heron in their cypress grove. These are some of the happenings that mark the happy hours at Tor House.

Ella Young, the Irish poet and folklorist, often came to Tor House in former years. She was a lovely ethereal person whose daily companions were the spirits of earth and air. One afternoon she had gone with Una and a passing visitor to Una's tower-room, and then to the top of the turret. They were watching a ship rounding Point Lobos when they heard two sweet chords of music several times repeated. The visitor said, "Robinson Jeffers must be playing the little organ"; unaware how impossible a suggestion that was. Ella, veil-enwrapped like a Druidess, said casually, "I often hear fairy music among the stones around this place." Una knows of no other explanation.

It seems so paradoxical a thing to say a poet has no ear for music, when such a poet as Robin *makes* rare music with his words. But it is true of him nevertheless, as of Yeats, who, his sister said, "couldn't carry a tune." Yet when Una plays one of her melodies in the candle light, filling the room with the haunting Gaelic music, Robin is always pleased. I sometimes wonder if he *hears*, or if he is only loving Una through his eyes as she sings.[38]

Recently, when the twins were home for a holiday from college, Una went to the organ and played some ancient Irish music for them which a friend had just sent her. Robin turned to Garth, smiling, "Don't you think that is a little better than your hill-billy music?" Garth said, "When we were little and mother played away on the organ in the attic while we were going to sleep, I never could tell whether it was the wind I was hearing, or mother and the organ."[39]

There is something continuously inspirational about Una's household. What is there, of course, is a harmony of home-and-family of an almost incredible perfection. She manages to make the routine of life an endless adventure!

During all the years Una has been married to Robin she has never had a servant, preferring to use that money for other things. For buying more land around their beautiful place, for trips to Ireland, for the boys' college. But hearing that old Fi, her little seamstress, was on the verge of losing her eyesight, Una invited her up to Carmel, thinking the change would be beneficial, and she could feel useful helping with housework and babies. "Fi," as everyone called her, acted like one demented. She made strange faces when referring to "this here *Caramel*," completely convinced that Carmel was a mad-hatter's village, entirely lacking in sanity of any kind. Fi greatly admired Una, but she had known her in the early days when she lived a totally different sort of life with Edward.

To say that the dear old lady was bewildered and skeptical about Robin is putting it mildly.

She thought him unbelievably strange. And when he sat up until four or five in the morning, writing poetry, with a huge goblet of Angelica wine within reach, her wildest fears were obviously justified. An amusing incident occurred one night when Robin, after hours of work, reached for his glass and found it empty.[40] Since Una had put the demijohn of wine away in the closet of her bedroom, Robin went in to get it. Not wishing to waken Una by lighting a lamp, Robin tiptoed into the dark room. As luck would have it, he bumped into a chair and knocked it over. It made a terrific crash, and of course poor Fi wakened and lay shuddering and shaking in her bed, fearing the worst.

Very early the next morning she rushed into Una's room. She was in a state of frenzy. "I'll testify for you in any court at any time, Mrs. Jeffers."

Completely mystified, Una demanded to know what on earth Fi was talking about.

"Oh, I heard it all when Mr. Jeffers tried to kill you in the middle of the night!"

It was all poor Una could do to keep her face straight. Afterwards when she told Robin he was greatly amused. Dear, gentle Robin who wouldn't kill a pigeon.

This is the poem that Robin was writing that night:

### THE EXCESSES OF GOD

Is it not by His high superfluousness we know
Our God? For to equal a need
Is natural, animal, mineral; but to fling
Rainbows over the rain
And beauty above the moon and secret rainbows
On the domes of deep sea-shells,
And make the necessary embrace of breeding
Beautiful also as fire,
Not even the weeds to multiply without blossom
Nor the birds without music,
There is the great humaneness at heart of things,
The extravagant kindness, the fountain
Humanity understands, and would flow likewise
If power and desire were perch-mates.

Those were unforgettable evenings when Robin read aloud to us. There were only a few times that he ever read his own poems. He thought he read them very badly, but Una would stop her

*Garth, Robinson, Donnan, and Una*

sewing and listen. She always sat in the same chair by the table in front of the fireplace, with a green eye shade she always wore when sewing, or making the little moccasins.[41]

Robin read often from Wordsworth and the Oxford Book of Verse. But I think the works of the Irish Renaissance were their great favorites at that period. Una loves Ireland and its poets passionately. There is probably no living person today who knows Yeats' works as Una does.

I know that Robin has been deeply influenced by the Irish mystics.

*Tor House and Hawk Tower with Jeffers and Sons on Turret, c. 1927*

It is interesting to know that Una never advises anyone how to live his life; she never criticises. She feels this is too great a responsibility to undertake.[42]

"If people have character and stability within themselves, they will go ahead in their own true life. If they don't I don't want to be bothered with them." With all her universal love of people subjectively, she has no sympathy with those of the dull eye and mind. She turns her back, abruptly, decisively, on anyone who bores her. She says, "I am too impatient, but what a gift Lincoln Steffens had for encouraging people—it was his best contribution to life. He could discern the most hidden talent and adjure you to drag it out into the light."[43]

Robin and Una have a great love and understanding of dogs. Billy, their great English bull, was just another member of the Jeffers family. Una owned Billy long before she married Robin. He lived to be fourteen years old.

Some friends examining the log cabin one day, asked me who *B. Jeffers* was. They had found the initials cut into one of the porch logs: "Una J.," "R. J." and "B. J." Those same initials are still there today, but poor Billy has long since died.

After the twins were born Billy included them in his small circle of devotion. His only way of expressing his fondness for Garth and Donnan was to knock them down clumsily but effectively. This used to alarm Una. Hearing sudden squeals and howls from the next room she would come flying to their rescue, and Billy would hurry to sit in his own chair when he heard her coming.

Whenever we took the twins riding in their express wagon Billy always came puffing along up the trails. Garth and Donnan loved these excursions as much as Billy did. They sat facing each other in the wagon and would laugh and gurgle at Billy's antics.

Billy was a genius at discovering a cool spot ahead of us on some trail. He would confiscate it triumphantly and wait for us to catch up with him. Then, very pleased with himself, he never failed to move to one side making room for all of us to rest.

His favorite trip, the place Billy liked most to go, was over to the dairyman's at Del Monte, where Una went every day to get fresh milk for the boys. Billy would rush feverishly from one end of the rear seat of the car to the other, stampeding the twins in his rapid shiftings.

The day Billy died the house was plunged into mourning.[44] Billy always kept guard while the youngsters slept, but this day he died while the boys were asleep. When they awoke Una bundled them into the car before they missed him. Nearing the top of the hill on the way to Monterey, Una and Robin heard the twins gurgling and talking their lingo together. Una turned and said: "What are you boys doing? What are you pointing at?"

And they answered gleefully, "Billy is outside on the road, running along and laughing at us. . . ."

They were leaning over the side of the car, following with their eyes something invisible to their parents. Poor, squat Billy, living had never been able to run beside a car! Presently Garth and Donnan began to play and wrestle and Una said quietly,

"Is Billy still laughing?"

"No, now Billy's away,"—their childish inconsequence undisturbed.

Una and Robin speak of this as their one authentic psychical experience; all the circumstances connected with the episode left no doubt in their minds that for a brief moment at least, Death had not been able to tear the apparition of their dear dog away from them.

After Billy died Una didn't want another dog, but finally Mabel Luhan gave her an adorable puppy, a pedigreed English bulldog called Haig, and Una lost her heart to him at once. He was so like the other that people marvelled because "Billy" never grew any older. In the market one day an old resident of Carmel saw Haig sitting patiently waiting for Una to finish her shopping; he came up and said, "My, my, Mrs. Jeffers, that dog never changes—hasn't grown a day older in all these years!"

Haig is so very much like Billy. I spoke to Robin about it one day, wondering if they came from the same family.[45]

Robin said, "No, it's just Una's tenderness. She makes boobies of all her bulldogs—and perhaps her men too!"

Haig lies before the fireplace, snorting and snoring in great contentment. His heavy breath jars the flames when he gets too close to the fire. Sometimes crackling bits will fly out and Haig, terrified, jumps up, stares about wildly, then lies down again. As the fire turns to coals Haig moves closer and closer until he is almost *in* the ashes. Una laughs as she watches this performance and says, "Haig and his wife."

It is incredibly droll to see Robin standing, anchored down by Haig at the end of his leash. Great, tall, silent Robin and squat, fat, noisy Haig. It is even funnier to watch Robin put Haig into his night shirt when it's bedtime. This ridiculous garment is a faded, disreputable thing vaguely resembling something that might have been once upon a time a knitted bathing suit or else a sweat shirt.

Una spreads a special cover on the foot of her bed and there Haig sleeps every night, Una serenely undisturbed by his snoring which grows so noisy it almost drowns out the sound of the sea.

Una said, "Last night I woke up to see Robin slipping out of bed very quietly. I asked him where he was going and he said, 'Haig pushed me out. I don't want to go but what else can I do?'

"'Gracious—why didn't you put Haig out?' I asked.

"'I don't know, it just never occurred to me to do it!' Robin said plaintively."

It used to become a romantic adventure, riding around Monterey —on back streets—up side streets—into grubby, indifferent old shops. Una was always in search of beauty. It never failed to delight her when she found a rare moonstone, or some other lovely reminiscent piece of jewelry.[46]

The antique stores in Monterey offered up strange argosies of poetical jewelry.[47] Una was invariably captivated—her imagination ran riot, finding stories to match her "finds." If the owner of the shop was reluctant about talking, Una was diabolically sly in ferreting out the different pathetic little histories which she instinctively *knew* belonged to the things she bought.[48]

There was a sad, strange woman living in Carmel, one of many transitory souls who came there eternally seeking solace of some sort. She was a Hungarian, and separated from her husband, a University of California professor. Una heard in some roundabout fashion that she wanted to sell some garnets. It was reported to be an exceptionally beautiful collection. So off we started in search of the lady. The twins went with us on this particular trip. I bought a bracelet for Una and a locket for myself. The locket has been lost these many years, but Una still treasures her bracelet.

Outside the woman's gate little Garth looked up and said, "Mother, why does that lady make me feel like crying?"

"She is so sad because she is far from her home across the sea, and, most of all, because she cannot see her little son."

Sometimes in the evenings I would sing for Una and Robin, and play my own accompaniments on the old square piano Una had bought in Monterey.[49] Its tone was faint and brittle—just right, she said, "for playing Scarlatti and little toccatas." Robin wrote a poem about that piano:

> Whose fingers wore your ivory keys
> So thin. . . as tempest and tide flow
> Some pearly shell, the castaway
> Of indefatigable seas
> On a low shingle far away. . .
> You will not tell, we cannot know.

Later I studied various things—Greek mythology, voice, piano. Presently I opened a studio and taught dancing. I worked long hours, hoping to forget the hurt of disillusionment. It was during this period that Edward and I were divorced. A year or two later

*Dining Room of Tor House*

I married Jim Greenan and we moved to the Orient. I tried so desperately never to lose Una. When my babies were born we exchanged many letters.[50]

Una once wrote, "I can't help but admire you for the way you have taken hold of your task. I can but sigh for you and your labors, for I too, have worked hard."

I didn't realize what I had done then but I do now; I had given up my dreams of a career and turned the dreams into an intimate reality. I found myself eager to create a home, eager for children. I, too, was willing to wash and cook and sew, since it was at that time a necessity.

I was again hoping to be like Una, praying for a fulfillment such as she possessed.

There were moments, *hours* of dread sorrow when I felt so inadequate without Una's laughing voice guiding me.

One night a strange thing happened. It was a sultry, foreboding night in the Philippines, the air heavy with jasmine and cereus and other unknown night-blooming flowers. The tribal gongs of the Igorots had been pounding for days and nights. The very air vibrated with their sinister, incessant sound. Their tribal dance was going on some place in the jungle. My head ached—every beat of those gongs intensified the pain. Even my heart kept pace.

Quite suddenly Una appeared before me. She smiled as she sat there, suggested moods for my interpretation of *Héloïse and Abélard.* I reached for a white scarf and draped it around my head, nun-fashion. I remember I walked away from Una into the garden, telling the beads and dreaming of Abelard. Una came with me, she appeared to be quite delighted. . . .

The sound of the gongs rose to an abrupt crescendo and Una vanished, but I had a feverish, curious feeling as though the whole hallucination had come as a warning. I knew then it was imperative to find my beloved friend once again.

When I did return after being away for ten years, I went instantly to Carmel to see Una. From others I was always hearing of her charm and wit, her poise and intelligence. I heard how she had helped Robin in his work, he was ever encompassed by her solicitude and tenderness and inspiration. Others knew her for these things, and will always—her place is secure by her influence on his work; but I was not seeking out the wife of a famous man —I wanted only to sit face to face and clasp the hand of my dearest friend.

And there I found her, in Tor House, just as inspiring as ever. Nothing had changed except to grow more beautiful. Robin had finished hauling rocks up from the sea. Hawk Tower was complete with white fat pigeons flying around it and nestling in its windows. They were using the big dining room now, which looked so like an old English inn kitchen, big fireplace, pottery of cheerful colors, little Chelsea figures beside the brass candlesticks, heavy oaken benches and pale rose, tiled floor, the rough tiles made and laid by Spanish workmen.

*Tor House and Hawk Tower*

Una still used the oil lamps and candles, the same Botticelli Madonnas smiled down from the redwood walls as serene as Una herself. There were hundreds more books piled up on top of everything—everywhere, on benches, on window sills, on new shelves reaching to the ceiling, books about things that interested her most—travel, biography, psychology, Irish archeology. . . . Poetry of course—"Do you know Rilke—his *Sonnets to Orpheus* —and have you read these marvelous 'New Poems' of Frederick Mortimer Clapp—our Timmie? You must. Now listen!"

There were the same shadowy mirrors, reflecting the sea and the flash of pigeons' wings in the courtyard. Oh, and in the pistol cupboard a skull, "such a nice one, with two teeth," and a carved wood image of the Cerne Giant displaying all his virility. A haze of sandalwood incense still floated up from the antique bronze burner, and there was the Steinway grand by the sea-window, and reed-organs—three of them! More than ever,

> . . . all a-sheenen
> Wi' long years o' handlen.

And there was Robin, world famous now, sitting by the fire, smoking his pipe, just as silent as always.

Only the twins had changed. They had grown up and been to college—handsome husky lads, who swaggered a bit, and shouldered their mother about like young oxen. Sometimes they took her dancing. She loved that. "It's a dreary thought," she says, "that they are grown up and must go away and make careers of their own. But I don't have to look back and regret that I didn't realize how happy I was while they were always with us—I blessed my happiness every day."

And the trees Robin had planted in 1919—they were so tall they touched the stars. . . .

Haig thought he remembered me and grew so excited in his greeting he proceeded to lose his dinner then and there. Robin laughed—"Haig has a demonstrative nature—he's so glad to see you, Edith."

In the evening, with her long braids hanging down over that Madonna-blue dressing-gown I had chosen for her in Shanghai, Una sat and played old airs on her organ. "Edith, this very one was found in Queen Elizabeth's Virginal Book. Actually it was written for the lute . . . but hear . . . ." Or else, "Can you realize that Petrie collected more than two thousand unprinted Gaelic airs? Just imagine what fun he had . . ." and off she'd be on one of her favorite topics.

But soon she would blow out the candle that lighted her music and open the drawer of that old mahogany dresser to reach for her gigantic white comb. ("I'm certain she found it," says Robin, "in a cave in the Orkneys. —Viking, you know—or worse!") She felt romantic, she *looked* romantic . . . but then she would cease to comb those long locks—I had seen her comb them a thousand times—she would cease and say: "If you *must* know the secret of that marvelous gingerbread we have for tea—it's sour cream. Sour cream does it." Or, "Robin, you've *got* to stop feeding the pigeons and quail every time you go into the courtyard. They are so fat their wings can scarcely lift them. Besides, one hundredweight of grain a month is all we can allot to *that* luxury. You know you promised. . . ."

Una took me into the little bedroom downstairs, off from the living room. It was very strange. Time had stood still here. My years in the Orient, the birth of my children, joys and pains—all my varied experiences sank away deep in my mind. I had circled back and all was unchanged; all was as I had remembered. The fire blazed on the hearth; there was the big bed by the sea window, and hanging from the beam above it a ship's bell, set under a teak-wood bar, copied from the one in Dürer's *Melancolia*. This bell has served one way and another in Una's family for over a hundred years. Now again I could reach up the moment I waked and pull the rope, and hear the immediate answering clang from Una's bell upstairs. As I undressed I read the words painted on the beam —Spenser's lines—

> Sleepe after toyle, port after stormie seas,
> Ease after warre, death after life, does greatly please.

Here was my port. Here I could rest secure, my nostalgia gone. It was all more beautiful than ever. Tomorrow I would rise up from sleep and decipher again these mottoes which Una used for solace and excitement. Robin had laboriously printed them in Gothic lettering, anywhere her eye would pick them up as she hastened to and fro about her work.

> The redie mind regardeth never toyle,
> But still is prest t'accomplish heartes intent. . .

That's a long hard one, from Alton Towers in Staffordshire. I like best, "Time and I against any Two." But this is Una's favorite:

> "Ffight on, my men," sayes Sir Andrew Bartton,
> "I am hurt, but I am not slaine;
> I'le lay mee downe and bleede awhile,
> And then I'le rise and ffight againe."

Tomorrow, too, we would climb to the little oak-paneled room in the tower, and tell our souls as we sat by the fragrant pitch-pine fire. Perhaps Una would play on the little melodeon up there, "Westron Wind," or "And how should I your true love know?"

Then I will bring out some phonograph records and improvise dances to them: blues, Hawaiian dances, and hot throbbing tangoes . . . and she will say, "Not too many of those, they are too exciting if I am just making shirts. Wait until I have to do something energetic—scrubbing maybe!"

Many of these memories are of years long gone by. The pattern of life changes fast, but there will be other lovely designs. Now my family and I are living in Carmel and are building a house on the mesa above the Mission. The many books that Una gave me, each with its evocative inscription, and Robin's books, shall have a shelf of their own in my living room amid other treasures of mine. There will hang the portrait of my grandmother with its sweet direct gaze. It was painted in China. An Oriental artist made this amazing likeness of her from a photograph my grandfather took out there with him.

Now I have three children: Maeve "of the lucky eyes and high heart," named after Una's first-born, Maeve so aware of natural beauty and sympathetic to my every mood. There is Jimmy with his care-free smile, happiest when some mischief is afoot; and my youngest, Owen, so much a part of me and my earlier dreams. To them I am dedicating this little book. It will help them to envisage a very real part of my life.

And how shall I end these memories? Perhaps best with this episode of two years ago, which began in imagined discord but ended on a true full note.

Some foolish person repeated a random, fragmentary bit of conversation, one of those destructive bits of gossip which are rampant in Carmel as well as in mining camps from Nevada to the Orient. I was deeply hurt. I couldn't bring myself to believe that Una had betrayed me knowingly, but I was determined to get to the bottom of the thing and find out for myself. There is no telephone in Tor House, so I was unable to call first. I just burst in upon her most unceremoniously. I found Una in the kitchen, in the throes of cooking an omelette. It was a decidedly inopportune moment. She was terribly cross with Garth for he had just been arrested for reckless driving. He and Donnan were in the dining room with two or three of their friends. They were laughing and talking and Una was fuming.

Besides this she confided, "There's a man in there with Robin in the living room. They're drinking my bottle of wonderful Scotch the Clapps gave me for my birthday. It's Arthur Hobhouse, M. P.!"

"What does that matter?" I asked, unimpressed, anxious to talk over my great trouble.

"Matter?" Una's voice rose to a shout as she started to beat up a bowl full of egg whites. "He's actually related to John Cam Hobhouse, Byron's Hobhouse! He's been here all day. We've been talking for hours about Lord Byron and the Abdication of the King, and English politics.

"We took him out to Point Lobos and kept him there until almost dark. When we came home I said, 'All we're going to have for supper is an omelette, you can stay if you like—omelettes are my great specialty,'—So he stayed!"

"How did you learn to make omelettes?" I asked irrelevantly.

"From a French novel." Una giggled and poured us both out some sherry. "I used to think I'd get a salon together by being famous for my omelettes."

"That's all very interesting," I said, "but I've got to talk to you right now!"

"Wait until I finish this omelette, Edith," implored Una. "Almost any moment can be fatal!"

"Well, this moment is fatal to me!" I said angrily.

"Oh dear, go in with Robin and Hobhouse *until* I get this thing finished—go trade this awful sherry for that beautiful Scotch."

Una was so insistent I went in to follow instructions, but Mr. Hobhouse refused to trade. He said very firmly, "No!" I went back and reported his deplorable selfishness.

By this time, due to my interference and Una's amusing conversation, the omelette had shrivelled up until it looked like a piece of old leather.

Una was terribly dismayed.

"Oh dear, look at it! And it's all I've got in the house to eat!"

But she didn't let this stop her. She placed it very daintily on a hot plate and carried it in on a tray to the M. P.'s chair. Then she came back to me and whispered triumphantly—"He's eating it, either politely or unconsciously!"

Then I poured out my heartache to Una. It was an idiotically inappropriate moment for a heart to heart talk but we had one nevertheless. Una explained what *had* been said and I was happier. I tried to explain my hurt feelings and how much I loved her, and she hugged me and we both wept, and laughed, and then Una grew very serious for a moment: "Well, I guess it's as you say, Edith—no one has ever loved me as much as you do."

Tor House, Carmel, California
St. Patrick's Day, 1939

Dearest Edith:

I have just finished reading your Ms. and a flood of memories sweeps over me. I had been saving these treasures for a later, quieter time. You've made me stop and look at some of them now, my "invisible landscapes" as Edgar Lee Masters calls them. He describes a place lived in year after year: the seasons revolve, sunshine and darkness cover it in turn, snow and rain fall upon the ever-changing human figures, until at last on that one field landscapes lie in layers like heaped-up leaves. We have that here at Tor House, that rich accretion, but if the wind blows through the leaves, if Edith thrusts in her hand and shifts them or if, as happened yesterday, I chance upon an old snapshot, how fresh and inviolate some scene, long-hidden, emerges. Here is the picture I found. You see that the day is gray and the wind flaps my old Paisley shawl as Robin and I say good-bye to a group of people at the gate. Across the courtyard two little boys are running, legs flying, bodies bent forward—the arrested movement of a split-second. My heart near burst as I looked at it—ah, the million darling, darling games Garth and Donnan are playing out there in our invisible landscapes!

You thank us for much happiness in those early days but you do not speak of the pleasure we felt in your eager delight and wish to participate in our daily life, and in your beauty, which was growing year by year. You stepped into your place by my side so naturally, for you were precisely the age of my twin sisters. It was I who had taught them to read and had been handing on to them ever after, books, names, Stars! Oh, I hope, my dear, I never arrived at the point of shaking you, did I?—as I shook Violet. I had come to suspect that girl's easy acceptance of the shapes that I pointed out in the constellations, however intricate or improbable they seemed. Suddenly one night I said, "Diagram that one!" and what she drew had no form—it was just a tangled *mess* of stars—I couldn't bear it!

I like your feeling about Tor House. Have you been reading

*Remembrance of Things Past?* for you are using Tor House as Proust did his grandmother, "the single constant value which makes the rest of the system possible," giving reality and significance to the general incoherent flux of events. I hope Tor House will always be that symbol of stability to you no matter how scenes and moods change and whirl about you.

Dearest Edith, still after twenty-six years,

Always faithfully,
Una

# THE MOUNTAIN VILLAGE

## (To U. J.)

### I

My adored and I have wandered from the flock,
We have taken up our love in our four hands
And carried it beyond the shadow of time.

Who are you, entering with calm tired faces
This mountain village of eternity?

She is my dearly loved and I am hers.
See, we have carried our most costly thing
Across the valley from the farther heights,
And brought it, villagers, for you to bless.

### II

Look down from the high village my adored,
Even from the village gate. A little while
Forget the kindly people gathered here
About us, and their calm and radiant eyes.
Forget the little houses though each one
Is beautiful, and every vine-bound door
Wide open to the olive-shaded street,
And the windows full of lilies. But look down
Over the white lake of the billowing mist
That bent above us for a cloudy sky
When we were crossing the valley. There the roar
Of tireless thunder and his leaping light,
Continuously aflutter like wild birds
Trapped in a vaulting, terrified our steps.
But here above that heaven is audible
No murmur of him nor a flash beheld.

### III

Look down from the high village my adored,
Even from the village gate, and say what forms
Move on the ridge beyond the ocean of mist.

A marching like a multitude of men
Moves on the farther ridge against the cloud.

Tell us you gentle-voiced calm villagers,
What is the file and multitude of men
That move on the ridge there against the cloud?

But you have come from there, do you not know?

Is it from there we have come? Indeed we knew
People must labor in the travelling world.
But yet it is most strange . . . yonder I see
Men who were dead before these wars began,
And look they are moved along the mountain-ridge
Upright and blithe, free travellers. To the right
Of the tall peak they walk, but on its left
Are men who never yet have lived on earth.
Yes. But regard more carefully the peak
Of which you have spoken.
                                        It is like a giant
Who holds a lantern over the moving heads.
So when I lived beside the blue Swiss lake
And near Geneva, we would often look
Up the long furrow of the swift Arve, to see
Napoleon's face carved on supreme Mont Blanc,
(They said it was) under the flame-white stress
Of the sun and glare of that ethereal world:
And so this peak appears to have the form
Of an old giant, and as the glaciers melt
In the afternoon on high mountains, so from him
The spittle and rheum of his extreme old age
From huge white points and fibres of his beard
Drizzle, and the lantern shakes in his old hand.

This is the watchman, that old giant Time.
Who turns as the long file flows under him
His sombre, thin and painful lantern-rays
On all the generations of the world.
His office is a watchman's and no more,
He does not move nor change nor make nor slay,
But only watches, holding with slow hand
His lantern over the reluctant heads.

IV

But those we have seen die are moving there!
My father whom I loved and have seen die
Walks the great ridge over the cloudy gulf;
My father; on the giant's right he walks,
Calm and slow-pacing as he used to be.

You saw the spirit struggle away from him.
The spirit alone is mortal, with its pains
And hopes and envious folly and vile fear.
Momentary reflection of that light
Time holds above the proud and passive world,
Flicker of the old lantern on some form,
And leaves it when it goes beyond that glare
Into the quiet of eternity.

The spirit is momentary, the being remains
Eternal and not spoiled?
                    You have understood.
His lantern is the mother of the hours,
And of all years and ages, but equally
Of the weak human spirit that shines and dies.

Then hope and fear, and joy and pain, are all
Contemptible?
                    At least we villagers
Believe so and are delivered from their teeth.

# V

Look down from this high village my adored,
Even from the village gate.

                              In little plots
The vineyards and the grain fields down the slope
Lie green and golden, delicate rills divide them
With silvery gush and whisper, then begin
The vast heads of the interbranching trees
Of that old forest we have wandered in.
Roofed and huge towers, but from so high beheld
They seem low lichen on an old gray stone.
They are somber and dense and starless; and a fog
Floods all the rest unto the farther ridge.

We must return unto the farther ridge.
The movement and necessity of things
Require us, we must march with multitudes
And labor in the giant's lantern-light.

But having carried our most costly thing
Up to this mountain village, even our love,
We walk with confidence and securely now,
The kindly villagers will keep it for us.

Here in the mountains of eternity
Dear villagers guard well your sacred trust.

CARMEL, 1916.

OF UNA JEFFERS

*Una and Edith with manuscript of "Of Una Jeffers,"* 1940

# Of Una Jeffers

## Selections from an Early Draft

In addition to the final typescript of *Of Una Jeffers*, an early draft of the manuscript is kept in the Greenan family archives. The early draft, also typed, contains a number of handwritten additions and corrections—some by Una, some by Edith, and a large number by Edith's daughter, Maeve. The latter were made many years after *Of Una Jeffers* was published—when Edith, living in Sacramento with Maeve, hoped to produce a new edition of her book. Maeve, in collaboration with her mother, worked through the manuscript. Together, they made small changes, primarily in syntax, diction, and grammar.

Selections from this draft are provided in the following pages. Though the published version should be considered normative—for only it was approved by everyone concerned—the early draft is very instructive. It contains an abundance of information that was cut from or changed in the final edition. Numbers preceding the passages correspond to notes in the main text, where the published version of an anecdote can be found. Or, vice versa, the notes in the main text indicate the existence of an earlier version of an anecdote, found here.

In most cases, the edited version of a passage is the one transcribed. In a few instances, however, where Edith's corrections are unclear or logic otherwise dictates, deleted or omitted words are recovered and inserted. Though spelling and punctuation are generally reproduced as written, there are a few very slight corrections—such as changing "St. Dennis" to "St. Denis" (as it appears in the published version) and moving a comma from after to before a concluding quotation mark.

1.  Edward Kuster, my fiance, was at the wheel of the "Yellow Peril," specially built at the Stoddard-Dayton plant in early streamlined magnificence, painted a deep cream with elegant brass fittings that glittered as we rounded the last curve and rushed inexorably into the driveway and on up to the house.

2.  Edward Kuster and I scampered up the stone steps for shelter from the slanting downpour and hesitated on the covered landing before dropping the knocker. I was closer to wilting than being refreshed by the trickling drops that glistened on my face for I was about to meet a dazzling personality. . . .

3.  She reached with a protective air for the long yellow driving gloves Edward was wearing and carried them with an air of fondness to the fireplace. They dripped the collected dampness into little pools upon the hearth, standing from the cuff-ends like desperate hands in prayer, or such was what I felt inside my nervously aware self. That manner of approach, that charm with which she took those yellow gloves and with daintiness placed them to dry was the first act that I ever saw emanate from this person who was later to become a dominating force in my life.

4.  I was tongue-tied, eager to drop something impressive into the give-and-take of this brilliant talk, but I couldn't fit in fast enough and by the time that I had desperately formulated a well-ordered phrase, they had swept on, leaving me to helplessly admire the figure at the center of the stage.

5.  . . . and she made adjectives pungent at times or as descriptive as the words themselves with tiny gestures of her fingers. She spoke of European reminiscences in a manner which I found to be her very own, shaping the carefully-selected phrases with her lips as if feeling the words as they left her.

6. She wore an Empire gown of black velvet of her own design. The high-waisted and puffed sleeves gave her an air of being transposed from some exciting period in history, an air which was enhanced by the dark brown hair, rich with deep tones of red, wound in braids about her head.

7. She moved to a chair and I quietly watched her and noticed that her very white skin had a radiance about it like pale alabaster through which light pours, or perhaps it was of the magnolia blossom texture.

8. She wore a medium length string of beautifully cut amber beads, and a matching topaz bracelet and ring set in old gold designs, of some long-remembered past.

9. As I grew closer to her the perfume of sandalwood emanated from the coils of her hair. When I came to know her well, she told me that sandalwood was something of her very own, that it had a loveliness that few women outside the Orient know. At that time she secured it from a small shop in the east, at moderate expense. Forever after, the odor of sandalwood brings Una before me as she was that damp night in Los Angeles.

10. It was a short meeting, yet it impressed me with the rhythm of friendliness that existed in the group. Among the snatches of conversation I gathered that Fanny was somewhat disappointed at the fact of the divorce that was then proceeding in legal orderliness between Una and Edward Kuster.

11. I gathered that "Fan" did not particularly appreciate Robin, for she could see in him little parlor charm. Robin was silent almost the whole evening, perhaps because he did not want to talk or because Una was doing most of it for him. Small talk has never been a part of Robin's life, I came to realize later. He never had had to resort to it in his own household and now he did not realize that this silence was brooding upon his hostess' mind. . . .

I spoke to Robin a few times and when he replied with more than a nod the answer was in a low voice, which came from him with great hesitation. The words were few, and the rare smile which attempted to lighten his face usually died before maturity as if it were sustained just long enough to make his condensed phrase satisfactory to the questioner.

12. He looked Lincolnesque—his high cheek-boned face beautifully rugged, tall, lean, rangy, with the greatest of restraint in every move he made. There was a direct, piercing, mesmeric look from his eyes that were sometimes violet, then blue, then blue-gray, as he sat there with very little to say. He seemed so distant and within himself and apparently he saw little need to come forth from his remoteness.

13. The evening was noteworthy to me for it was my first meeting with Robin, and another spent with Una and I learned more of her, for I gauged my every remark in an attempt to meet with her approval. I weighed each idea so that it might interest her, and from that evening I recall that I was so much impressed that I decided to model my life upon hers, that I would start out designing my own clothes, not copying Una's, but working out original ideas to suit my own self. I recall that on the next day I went forth in search of a perfume which would enhance my own personality, and would not be of any type resembling the sort found on most Los Angeles women.

14. Robin and Una were stopping with Robin's parents in South Pasadena. Una never had much of a liking for Southern California, for she adored to be nearer the hills and the ocean. She hated the drab monotony of residential regularity, the depressing listlessness of hot weather, and the dull routine of living without imagination, and she felt restricted when in towns and cities. But she liked the garden and the fruit trees about the Jeffers' home, and the comfortable, livable frame house with the tall shrubs about it. She was in sympathy with the simplicity of life behind those walls, the music, the books, and

the walks in the evening. This was all that really counted in Una's life then, for she had no desire for parties and people, but to have Robin with her, together in simple living was sufficient, and in this fullness of being together needed little else.

15. Robin's mother was a tall woman who carried herself proudly erect at all times, displaying a great dignity of bearing and grace. Her hair was then gradually graying. I saw her two or three times. She was quiet in her contacts, pleasantly friendly. Una always called her "Belle-Mère." There was in her a resigned acceptance of the situation that was being woven and she was gracious to all concerned, for she had great refinement and a background of education. She was quite an accomplished musician, for she had a good voice and played the piano and organ exceptionally well, and I have always felt that a great deal of her generous influence has had a strong hold upon Robin and yet it was she who said, after Robin and Una had married, that it was Una and Una alone who could bring her son to accomplishment. I can visualize her now in her graciousness and her radiant smile as she looked so sympathetically upon me.

16. After the battle Kinney was laid out in the drug store, and souvenir hunters snitched & tore remembrances from the bandit's body, even dipping handkerchiefs in his blood to be displayed later with much pride! It was a rowdy town which never seemed to acquire a veneer from its neighbor cities but remained a movie-set cowboy junction steeped in an aura of the West which was partly composed of Tiburcio Vasquez, Kinney, a club-footed bear, and of course the girls, the beautiful, exotic creatures of the red-light district! As we passed one on the street I remember asking my mother who that gorgeous lady was, so much more beautiful than the average housewife of that place & time. When a great fire burned down the tenderloin district, it seemed, although confined to that area, to wipe out the entire city.

17. These days of study with Ruth and Ted developed into a grand friendship, and Ruth St. Denis has played a memorable part in my life, always providing me something for the moments when I would turn to music and some inspiring fire would find myself reverberant with the rhythms of the dance . . . . There was a great dynamo within the artist that was Ruth St. Denis and her touch was a spell upon many of my friends who were also pioneers in the Denis-Shawn school. Ruth Austin, Martha Graham, Ada Forman, Betty Horst, Margaret Loomis, Doris Humphries, and the lovely Mary Hay, all were touched with that magic power that Miss Ruth alone could convey and I look today at these careers and can point toward that ephemeral quality that is there but always escaping the absolute touch of a commercial world.

Una knew Ruth and Ted and had many pleasant visits with them.

18. Later, when we were building a large house in San Gabriel, Una and Robin with the bulldog came to visit me. One time they arrived while the house was under course of construction and we talked of housebuilding but Una made no comment. Later, when this whole period had faded, she came to me frankly, "Tell me, Edith, you didn't expect to like San Gabriel, now did you?"

"No," I had to admit, "now I realize that I always hated it. But at the time I was too busy trying to do things with my life to know how much I really hated it." Una smiled knowingly. The whole episode was dreary, lonely, and arid, but during the time, of course, what with Ruth St. Denis' routine, the study list supplied by Una, as well as my willful attempts to soften the strained marital life which I was trying to put forward with ease from a stressed emotional background, I was too busy to notice.

Una knew that this marriage required a great deal, for she had been married to Ted Kuster for ten years, and perhaps, I was avoiding the direct issues and seeking release in the dance and in music, yet I felt too that I was in an altogether unsuitable locale. Una knew this very well, yet she would never bring it forth as advice, and so I was made to see it clearly for myself, and I finally saw it through.

19. After I married Edward Kuster, Robin and Una came several times to visit us in our cottage in La Jolla near the sea in Southern California. On one occasion, the four of us visited the San Diego Fair of 1915. It was a beautiful drive in the "Yellow Peril" and a completely enjoyable day of sightseeing.

As we crossed a high bridge over a deep ravine of tangled woodside, we noticed sauntering there a tall man of grace and dignity. Suddenly he stopped, stepped lightly to the rail, took a deep view of the beautiful surroundings and spat lustily. Robin, in high glee pointed to the movement done so grandly, and said, "He walked onto the bridge, looked, spat, and walked on," and roared again with amusement.

This Fair did not aim at the spectacular as the Panama-Pacific Exposition of the same year, but we, like four ridiculous children, had great pleasure in its informality. I remember the Pueblo Indians attempting light housekeeping in confined quarters, and the Fun House where Robin and Una burst into hysterical laughter as dignified ladies would suddenly be swirled off into space from a great roulette wheel. Of course, this after our own sudden pirouetting.

It was this same day, when toward evening we acquired a few sandwiches and took them to Laguna Beach on the way homeward. As we sat on the shore, I planted four little white candles about us in the sand, and when it grew chilly and we had to leave, the candles were left to burn. We watched them as we mounted the cliff to the roadway and as we drove along the shore there was a little glowing spot behind that inspired Robin to write me a poem later, saying "Lovely thought, dear friend, leaving those candles in the dusk, leaving them burning as we walked away."

20. Another day Edward and I were driving the Jeffers back to Pasadena in the "Yellow Peril." Una was very tired from the strenuous afternoon and I turned to see how she fared in the rear seat, and there she was, beaming out upon the landscape. "Why Una, I thought you were worn out." Robin answered for her, "Yes, she's awfully tired, but she's afraid she'll miss something and she won't close her eyes."

21. Una adored most animals except cats, and flies. She was certain that she would not like cats and kept constant vigil for the safety of her Bantam flock about Tor House.

Flies presented an easier problem for she could take a folded newspaper to the window, capture the intruders into the folds and dash them into the fireplace. And she did it with grace!

Once the twins were presented with a pair of lovebirds, and today there is a large flock of pigeons fluttering about the Hawk Tower . . . .

22. A few months later, after Una's first-born had died, the two of us were walking into La Jolla village, with Una's bulldog stomping at our heels. A lady passed who had known Una in earlier days when Robin and Una had lived there before Maeve was born. The two of them dropped back a pace and I could see the sadness creeping up into Una's eyes as she told of her loss, and when she returned to me I saw those rare tears clouding her eyes but within a few steps they were gone. We walked in silence until the uneasiness brought out from her, "One must always close the doors behind one."

23. I remember my first visit to Carmel, which became to Robin his *genius loci*, and is now known as Jeffers Country. A train ran as far as Monterey on the Peninsula. From there, in a sur-

rey drawn by horses driven [by] Tom Powers, there was a steep rise over a gradually increasing grade which became seeming unsurmountable for the poor team. Along the way there were vistas back upon old Monterey and its harbor. On top of the long grade, one waited while the horses rested and from there the track fell away to the sea—a realm of forest vagrancy with the blue sea at its base. With the horses again in prime, Tom Powers was off with his weight joggling about in his attempt to hold the hot wooden brakes in the steep descent of Ocean Avenue into Carmel. In those days the village had a few stores of the false-front variety, with the regular split-front for show-windows. L. S. Slevin combined stationery with the delivery of the Post and when the entire village would run to a fire or to the beach, the only person who was sure to be the guardian of the town was "Pop" Slevin, pioneer extraordinary.

Ocean Avenue then was a deep-rutted road that dropped away into disrepute as it fell into the chaparral on its way toward the beach, but, as I remember, it was fair as far as the old Pine Inn where I turned down a trail to Robin and Una's little log cabin which seemed lost from civilization of any kind, and yet Una assured me that there would be someone within shouting distance if one shouted loud enough. Just a few days before she said, she had been attracted across the Eucalyptus-filled ravine by a neighbor in wild declamations of some sort, and although Una could not hear clearly, she believed something wrong in her wild grimaces and gestures but later found it to be the home of Mary Austin and the novelist herself was testing a scene upon her stoop.

. . .The first time I arrived they met me in a surrey and the wheel became caught in the car tracks on Alvarado, the main street of Monterey, but Una, always impatient with such clumsy or stupid inconveniences, grimly proceeded with the wobbly wheel, completely indifferent to the ridiculous sight we must have presented to villagers.

24. I was often a visitor to the little log cabin in Carmel, and I believe I may have been one of Una's few friends who went there to stay, for it was a very small rustic cottage that half-slid down a gulch and seemed to hold to the little rain-washed embankment only for the sake of its occupants.

25. I spoke of the meal which she had served a short time before. I told how much I liked the simplicity of it, for Una had served it on the bare table top, cut from one log in a great slice. It was arranged without ornament, but it was cosy in its simplicity, for she had served it in thick yellow bowls creating for me an old-world interest, and later, in the warmth of the evening's fire, with the odor of sandalwood streaming from an antique burner, I felt a great part of the Jeffers household, for it was as a sister that I came to her and she has always reciprocated with a generosity of spirit which even a sisterly tie might not be always expected. That evening I recall the fire itself was lent a bit of Una for its brilliance as we had gathered the driftwood during the day along the shore. She would select the pieces that would burn with the most color, knowing full well the species of wood that burned more brightly than another. Then, on the shore, we would pile the logs together and sit on the sandbank, watching mechanical little sandpipers running back and forth with the ripples that scalloped the beach, or observe the great storm clouds hungering on the horizon. The driftwood we carried on our shoulders from the dunes through the cypress thicket to the log cabin, and in the evening the memory of the outing would glow before us in multi-colored flames.

26. One memorable evening when Robin asked Una to read Synge's "Riders to the Sea," and as the tragedy swelled the room in almost Grecian splendor, I could hear the tremor in her voice toward the close, and when the little play was completed, there were those rare tears burning in her eyes. Una had seen something beautiful, and they were not tears of grief

but of a great beauty that had swept above us, and we three sat in silence for many minutes after reflecting upon the dynamic little play.

There were many evenings of reading the works of the Irish Renaissance, and I feel that this great union of appreciation had a good deal in bringing Robin and Una together, and that this very movement that came so unexpectedly and has sustained itself so admirably in the realm of letters brought additional interest into their lives . . . .

I find these chords so often in the works of Robin that I know such great forces have touched him deeply. And when one realizes, the reader is often as much a creator of the illusion of the work in the resources that he brings forth to the writings, that in him is often found the fulfillment and the real purpose of the author. It is then that I realize that these evenings were great opportunities for me, for I could hear read by two great and appreciative minds, the works that almost seemed written for such as these . . . .

These evenings are never to be forgotten, and when I thought of writing of Una, it was of these evenings that I at first turned for I wanted to leave a little of the charm, a little of the friendly atmosphere that pervaded them, and if I have given a mere key of what I should like to record, the purpose which I set out to accomplish is gratifying. I never visited Una and Robin as New England ladies of the Nineteenth Century called upon Longfellow, and Emerson, and Holmes, and wrote of the gardens and the slope of the roofs, as my visits were as a member of the family coming for the comforts of old associations and to gain from two great counsellors a road back toward a goal which I had set for myself long ago in Bakersfield, a perfect harmony within myself.

27. One night we were about the fireplace, just Robin and Una and I, and we were cold from the draft that rushed about us

from the storm that beat on the little log cabin—when a white bird beat its wings at the window and Una told us of the Irish legend of ill-omen that would surely befall. We sat in silence for a few minutes reflecting. I recalled a play of Lady Gregory, but Una grappled with a new idea and thrust it upon us to take us away upon new thoughts.

28. Often, after a tea-time discussion we three, Robin, Una and myself, along with Billy the bulldog would wander to the water's edge where we would discuss my day's reading or the less vital incidents of the day and as the evening thickened about us, Una would pick out the constellations and endeavor to diagram them for me while Robin and Billy tracked along in our wake or dashed to some distant knoll and with a fury, would bound down to the beach. Una loved to see them running in the evening, down the dunes, a lanky man racing with a great bulldog down the crystal-white sand in the twilight.

29. We would frequently go into the hills for long walks and here I discovered the great familiarity Una had with every inch of the countryside, for she knew with intimacy the flowers by the path-side, the lupins that came in the spring and early summer and the tidy-tips and the baby-blue-eyes, and the Santa Cruz Iris, the poppies and at Point Joe the golden baeria and at the water's edge, the gray, red-tipped cotyledon on granite edges. Una very seldom picked the flowers for her preference seemed to be for bunches of uncommon wild grasses with fantastic pods, a scattering of odd stray blooms and the shaggy russet of Indian warrior. She would point out the birds to me on these long walks, the cormorants, the pelicans and the shearwaters along the shore, for in my inland childhood these were unfamiliar to me. From these walks I came to realize how much she loved this region and the great shafts of the Santa Lucia range farther south. She wrote to me on occasion of the Big Sur area, of its remoteness and inac-

cessibility. Robin and Una had taken their first trip down the coast by horses and wagon for the road then was a precarious one. It was on one of these early trips that they came upon the old ranch house which became the scene of one of Robin's great works. Una asked an old resident of the neighborhood of this abandoned homestead and he had told her that the last owner had been killed by his stallion. This became the nucleus for "Roan Stallion."

30. To probe the beauties that lay upon these hillsides seemed to be the task and the joy that Una had set for herself and she went about it with the mood and for me the unconscious charm of those who went into the English countryside of Hardy and the sisters Bronte, bringing home the sagas of her region, which she would warm from prosaic incidental to color and bring them into the light with personalized intensity.

31. After a day's trip through the hills, we would come home to the cabin and in the evenings, with Angelica wine before us, Robin would read to us from Shelley or a few fragments of the Irish mystics, but more often it would be from Shelley, or again the "Song of Solomon," and then we would talk of the day's adventures, perhaps it had been to Point Lobos by surrey, or to the honey-man's, to the brook for cress for the evening's salad, or to the woods for quiet reading. Lobos was a favorite trip. It reminds me of a Japanese print with its great chasms with dwarfed trees clinging to the crags and its great depths where the raging surf vibrates like the heights of a Wagnerian score. Nothing can take from me those walks on the precarious paths of Lobos with Robin and Una and Billy the bulldog.

Often on the homeward path we would slip down to the sea for a quick plunge near the mouth of the Carmel River. Una and Robin usually stood by and watched me, for Robin, although a great swimmer in college days and at Redondo

Beach and Palos Verdes, seldom swam in Carmel Bay, and Una preferred a pool to the cold breakers, although later she bathed in the sea every morning across from Tor House. Perhaps then she was frightened. I thought this later when Robin took the twins to the shore, letting them run into the breakers, for a mask of fear arose upon Una's face—in her horoscope there is a notation of the danger of water. I loved to dash about in the surf, embracing the great rolls of cool waters that fell over me in ecstatic profusion, for I felt as a dancer in the great robe of the elements, with the wind swirling and the waves splashing at my body and the tide pulling the sand from beneath my feet. I remember Robin saying of me one time as I emerged from the spray, "Edith, you skim the water like some beautiful seabird. I shall never go to the shore again without seeing a bacchante along the edge of the foam," and I recall these days with that tremendous joy of reminiscence when I re-read Robin's lyric "Fauna."

32. Una had a sense of making me feel secure in the most trying times of insecurity, of appeasing a forlorn hunger with a little narrative that glamorized food as it was served, or commenting on an incident in a way that would make a weary traveller drowsily happy. Each day would come to her as a new adventure and this spirit sould be so impressed on my own consciousness that I too would become a part of her plan and so we would go to the old man's in Carmel to fetch wild-flower honey for our breakfast cakes or scones for tea. Or we would take a surrey to Monterey with Una driving and saunter to Fisherman's Wharf and there we would go to the end of the wharf where Una would select a lusty salmon from the nets as they were being hauled in.

33. Una adored the simplicity of life, dependent upon the mere necessities of wholesome foods, and becoming clothes. She was always conscious of the utilitarian, and her only luxuries

were in the few objects of jewelry, never expensive, but always in perfect accord with her personality, and the lovely pieces of furniture that she had bought at low prices from furniture shops during days when authentic pieces were regarded as obstructions. She lived a very direct life and her wants were simple, for she did not care to clutter living to lose sight of its real purpose. She told me often that there were beauties in essentials, the divine normalcy, the stripping from the clustered encumbrances, and she, in her own pattern was one of the best exemplifications of it. "Magazines and phonograph records and other short routes," she said, "are often mere dissipations for the true benefits offered by books and finer music."

34. During this period Una placed me on a schedule of reading with a purpose, and I recall that on the list were the works of Barrie, the works of Poe, and d'Annunzio's "The Flame of Life," and several volumes of Irish legends, and as I was busily occupied with one book on her reading list, she turned to me from the well-thumbed copy of Swinburne, and she said very slowly, "Poetry, you will find, Edith, bears great fruit for living. Poetry is first, last, and all the time, for in it you will find something that is nowhere else in literature." She then paused reflectively and again took up her Swinburne and with a familiarity that needs no great concentration, read on for hours.

35. These were happy little outings, so unlike the times we had had in Southern California, for now it was in the intimacy of understanding. She had become my guide and would recommend to me books that I should read, and so I discovered the beauties of George Moore and W. H. Hudson and William Butler Yeats, and I read Arthur Symond's essay, "Wordsworth and Shelley," a copy of which Una had given Robin early in their friendship. I followed this with Dostoevski's "Crime and Punishment," then the Waverly novels, Cellini's Autobiography, the Arabia Deserta, Emerson's essays, in particular

"Self-Reliance," the verse of A. E., the verses of William Sharp who wrote under the pseudonym of Feona McCloud, for he indicates a great love for the sea so similar to Una's, and then there were many other works. I remember Una turning to me after I had become engrossed in a volume from her list, "Wasn't that a brilliant preface, Edith?" I think it was one of Shaw's plays, and I told her that I had overlooked the preliminary pages, so anxious was I to burst into the play itself, and she came back at me with "But, Edith, the book lover always reads the preface, for there is the stimulating beginning and it is all-important."

36. I remember now another incident of these days. Una was then anticipating the arrival of a new child which resulted in the twins, Garth and Donnan. During the period before their birth, Una confessed to me a mad craving for celery. She could attribute it to no cause, but whenever we were out the two of us would keep a weather eye for a cool market where the supply was fresh and unlimited. I can see her now with the long crisp stalks, and her Swinburne.

37. I went to Una. She had just finished bathing and rubbing them with oil. One of the twins looked pale with dark circles under his eyes. I wondered if it was good for her to undertake all of the duties with her great and fierce love and grimness, but I knew by this time that these qualities were a great part of her. Although taxed, she would go ahead, loving the great absorption.

After her close attendance while the twins were very young, I would join her and we would take long rides into the countryside behind Glendale while Belle-Mère or Robin baby sat. She possessed an old Ford that seemed to love to escape the city as much as we did. As soon as we left the suburbs, Una again seemed to be herself, for she was under the constant pressure of care in the daily welfare of her twins. She hated the valley sunshine and longed for the peace of the misty hills and the fog and the late moments of the day. I knew then that she was anxious to return to Carmel-by-the-Sea.

38. Robin seemed not to have an ear for music yet when Una would sound the rich chords on one of her reed organs, he was pleased. I have seen her so often playing there in the evenings at Tor House with her thick braids falling about her and the tones of some Elizabethan melody or Celtic ballad enveloping her like a great-cloak of another world and she seemed at the time very remote, yet after a time she would reach into a high-boy drawer, draw out a long comb and prepare herself for sleep, talking the while of how she made ginger-bread or how she kept the pigeons from coming too near the kitchen window.

39. Today, in her Tor House, Una has several diminutive organs, one in the living room, another upstairs, one in the tower-room of the Hawk Tower, and still one more that is to be carried about. Besides, there is a handsome Steinway grand before the windows overlooking Point Lobos and the sea. One evening I bravely took out with me a group of phonograph records including a number of vigorous band selections. Una said she loved the exuberance of the band numbers but found them demoralizing, for she knew that the possession of them would break into her household duties, for having them about would prevent her from listening to real music. For many years there was no radio in Tor House until one of their greatest friends, Noël Sullivan, gave one to the twins. Sullivan was a great student of Bach and was the inspiration of the famous Bach Festivals held in Carmel each summer. Of him I have often heard Una say, "Both Robin and I are tremendously fond of Noël. He is truly one of our best friends."

40. Una preferred Robin not to depend too heavily upon the wine to give him inspiration so she would limit him upon her

retirement to one night-cap goblet. This limitation brought about an amusing experience while I was there. Robin had been at work for several hours and with renewed vigor started work on a new poem. He found however that his glass was drained, and since Una had taken the demi-john with her to her bedroom, the only source of supply was from that direction. As he entered the bedroom he stumbled over some obstruction, a chair perhaps, and it crashed to the floor. Fi was terrified and did not sleep a wink the rest of the night. The first thing in the morning she rushed to Una and told her that if she had decided upon a divorce that she would be the first one to testify that Robin had attempted to kill her while she slept, "In any court, at any time," Fi answered Una. Mrs. Fifield never could understand these "writer-fellows."

41. I can still recall the evenings when we would sit about the fireplace and she would bring out soft leather strips and prepare to make moccasins for the twins and she would weave in the intricate pattern as deftly as a professional and they would result in smooth, comfortable little pairs which she would place on the mantlepiece. Robin would reach for some poetry of the classicists or, on a few memorable occasions, his own verse and in a quiet, low voice, almost a monotone, and barely moving his lips, voice his long narratives with the accents droning on to climactic passages and then the backdrop of the Santa Lucian mountains would dominate the scene, and the lives that had trespassed would quietly fade away into the great descriptive beauty of landscape; and then I realized that Robin was one of the few poets who make details of birds and flowers cling reverberantly to a landscape, and across that imperishable scene move characters into tremendous drama, and I knew that through Una he had gained a great familiarity with the district, which shall ever be a part of the Jeffers tradition.

And then of evenings Robin or Una would pour the rounds of Angelica from an opalescent five-gallon demi-john which had come from a dark, cool wine shop in Monterey. Robin cared very little for hard liquors. The wine was a smooth after-dinner pleasure, poured into water tumblers, and then it would be Robin's turn, or perhaps Una's, and one or the other would read from Wordsworth or the *Oxford Book of Verse*, Synge, whose "Riders to the Sea" was a great favorite, Padriac Colum, or other Irish plays and verse which meant so much to Una and was one of the important spheres which she brought to Robin. The preference was for Shelley, and when Robin would turn pages in his reading, he would glance up during the pause, looking deeply as if to say such beauties could touch a heart as his.

There were only a few times when Robin brought forth his own work, for he felt that something was lost in bringing into light compositions in progress, but when completed he could at times be prevailed upon to read them to us. Una, in silence would drop her duties and her head would fall forward and her eyes would be hidden by the green eye-shade she always wore when reading or sewing or darning or weaving the little moccasins before the firelight and the lamplight, in the quiet of the evening in our enchained and happy circle. It was a very close contact and I adored it for they were so patient with me and believed so thoroughly in me, and held that I had great promise, and when I read that Robin has used the phrase that Wordsworth wrote of his sister, Dorothy, that Una had given him eyes to see with, and ears to hear with, I have the same feeling that Una, in her turn, gave me eyes to see the beauties of life and nature, and ears to hear the loveliness that is all about one and it was she who could make from a dull existence a drama that always had its daily enlightenments; and I, perhaps under the red robe of discord, could return to the brilliant expectations that this life is always full of. But to be away from her, away from her loveliness and her great guiding counsel, made me afraid.

42. In her great warm manner, Una was never direct in her advice, never dominatingly possessive, but always with patient stress in pointing a way by telling of her own experiences, for she was always gracious when she was being helpful, as when I overheard Edward Kuster talking to Una, just after their divorce. Una said "From this point in my life, there will only be beauty," and Ted asked, "Do you mean friends? Friendships, Una?" And she turned and said, "No, only beauty," and then her eyes turned in sightless reflection and she added, "All my life I've closed doors so tightly that I couldn't open them if I wanted to."

Edward looked at her and said, "Perhaps fortunately?" I felt, a little bitterly. Una merely raised an eyebrow, smiled, and talked of other things.

43. There have been many who have come to her for her approval and suddenly become petrified with her disapproval. Una was really a great creative artist, but her medium was people. I have heard her say that the greatest thing Lincoln Steffens left behind was the real encouragement that he gave to those who came to him, and I have felt for many years that this same quality was dominant in Una.

44. I recall the gloom that came upon the household the day Billy died. He had always kept guard while the twins slept, but this day he had expired on a rug in the sleeping-room and without disturbing the boys, Una and Robin had removed the body and the rug. When the twins awoke, they asked for the dog and then asked why the rug had been taken out of their room. Una told them that it needed cleaning. With this, their suspicions diminished. That afternoon, on the way to the dairyman's, they asked again for Billy, for he had always ridden with them and the car showed visible signs on

the fenders where his spittle had rusted the paint. Una told them that Billy was running along the side of the car and she slowed up so that he could catch up.

45. Haig was so very much like Billy that I often remarked to Robin of the similarity for I have known both dogs well. I even noted that they acted alike. Robin assured me one time that there was something to it. "It is because we give Haig the same treatment and so, through environment, he has become a new Billy."

46. Jewelry was never worn by Una except when the gown she was wearing called for an accent, but she loved to have them about in little boxes ready for an occasion.

47. I recall the antique shops of Monterey where we would wander after completing our prosaic duties, such as grocery buying. In these musty corners we would become engrossed in old cases with bits from the Orient and oddities of no particular value, yet the histories of these little objects held great fascination for us. At that time, both Una and myself were entranced with garnets but, as good specimens were hard to find, most of these tours were in search of an old bracelet or locket or chain.

48. Una and I often wandered off to the back streets in search of the out-of-the-way jewelry shops, and she would scour a tray of remnants of another day. Seldom did she come away without a lovely pin with a semi-precious stone in an old setting, a lapis lazuli, which she adored for this stone brought out the loveliness of her eyes, yet she seldom wore jewelry except in the evenings and then her favorites were amber or topaz, or an old pin which she had picked up from somewhere. I asked her once about this particular piece, and she elaborated to the most minute particulars, descriptions of a shop in Rome, a dark alley in London or Dublin; and so intimate were her de-

scriptions of a clerk and his manner or the oddities hanging about, that it became almost an experience of my own. She loved jewelry, often merely to bring forth from a cupboard to show and to dangle about as she told their history, a few garnets in Victorian settings, a brooch from an antique store.

49. Too much stress can never be laid on the great gentleness of Robin's spirit, for although at times his writings are grim, stark and powerful, his personality to his friends was directly opposite, for he had a great gentleness, a sweetness and a kindness that I have never seen exhibited so continuously in anyone else. He was always kind and patient with me even when discussions ran deeply into subjects into which I had never delved, and when someone would probe me for a reaction to the subject under discussion and I would hesitate, Robin would quickly come to my rescue with "Don't interrupt her. She's thinking. She's listening," and he would look at me from his blue eyes with a whimsical smile.

I recall one evening when we had talked of books and came onto world conditions. Edward Kuster, by then my husband, introduced the argument of helping the masses, and he was opposed by Una. Una's point of view was that you can help one, but not the masses, and when they turned to me, I considered for a time and then hesitated. Robin rescued me, for he knew that at this point all concerned would readily accept a little diversion, so he asked with great diplomacy, "Would you sing, Edith?" So, with a quick look into the eyes of Edward and Una and without saying a word, I moved to the old square piano that Una had bought in Monterey. Una decorated it in the evenings with two lighted candles and Robin had given it further glamour by writing a poem of it,

> Whose fingers wore your ivory keys
> So thin—as tempest and tide-flow
> Some pearly shell, the castaway

Of indefatigable seas
On a low shingle far away—
You will not tell, we cannot know.

There were two favorite compositions which I would sing
to my own accompaniment, "Melisande in the Woods" and
"The Gypsy Trail," of "Follow the Romany Patteran, East
where the silence broods . . . ."

I cannot recall how many were the evenings when I would
sing for them or perform a few of my "attitudes" with a crim-
son shawl and then I felt like Lady Hamilton before their
courteous applause, but it was in no manor-house I per-
formed but in the timbered cabin of Carmel.

50. To Una, the dance was a great art, but there were other things
along her purposeful road, but to me at the time this was a
new and an important outlet and an accomplishment which
I felt had a distinct meaning, and Una was a wise guide but
she still insisted on my other assets that needed to be worked
to their fullest, and so I crammed into myself everything pos-
sible, perhaps for its own sake, but I excused it, hoping it might
be a meeting ground with my husband. I studied mythology
of the Greeks, music, voice and piano, and then I turned to
the dance again and opened my own studio in Los Angeles,
and then the pages of the years shifted by and my marriage
with Edward Kuster dissolved into respect and divorce and
my dance pupils absorbed my time and gave me a fullness
that only a daily task can give to one, and then I was happily
married again to the father of my children, and without the
purpose Una had inculcated into me paramount before my
eyes, I went into a complete reversal.

All that I had taken up with a will had to be dropped. I
had lost the key to my inner self. I began to drift, and with-
out Una in attendance, I fell away hopelessly, and my hus-
band, an important mining man, took me to the Orient, but

there I found the frivolities of social life quite as disastrous and the only anchorage I had was in my children, and being so far away from Una, I had no guidance except from her letters, and so when the children were young, I turned to metaphysics and psychology with Delphine Ashbough, who was a Dodge of Detroit, and a very remarkable lady. I recalled that while I had had a dancing academy, Miss Ashbough had come to see one of my prize pupils and when the child had completed the mood, Miss Ashbough turned to her secretary, Miss Beauvais, and said, "Where did that child learn to express sorrow so deeply?"

Later I reflected upon that remark many times. Perhaps I had instilled that dread sorrow that I had so often felt, and again saw coming when I found that the grasp was slowly slipping and that I was disintegrating into routine motherhood. Then suddenly, one tropic night in the Philippines when the Igorots were in the turmoil of a tribal dance and the gongs had been vibrating for days and I was in desperation with a head that seemed to split with each beat, there came to me Una as she sat before me suggesting moods for my interpretation of Eloise of "Eloise and Abelard," and I reached for a long silken white scarf and with it close about my head in nun-like fashion, I walked into the sultry garden telling the beads and dreaming of Abelard. It seemed as if a fever had overcome me, but I could feel his presence, the Abelard all entwined with Una's suggested movements and then, almost without moving, I turned and seemed to see a vision, and as I moved in fright, my hands dropped away and the headdress fell from me. It was a strange phenomenon, as if some conscience of an earlier day resurrecting itself had come that night to warn me never to lose that hold I had once had. I had been away from her, and when I returned, after being apart for ten years, I journeyed to Carmel with that purpose only in mind; and there was Una . . . .

*Una Jeffers*
by Johan Hagemeyer

# Illustrations

# Index